Introduction

In an ever-evolving digital landscape, where the competition for consumer attention is fierce, innovation is the cornerstone of successful marketing. Enter Video Marketing with AI—a cutting-edge fusion of visual storytelling and artificial intelligence that is revolutionising the way brands engage with their audiences. As AI technology becomes increasingly integrated into our daily lives, businesses are quick to capitalise on its vast capabilities, from data analytics to process automation. But nowhere is this intersection more potent or promising than in the realm of video marketing.

The benefits of deploying AI in video marketing are multifold. Beyond the sheer speed and efficiency that automation brings, AI offers a nuanced understanding of user behaviour, enabling the creation of personalised content that not only resonates but also delivers actionable insights. With its capacity for complex data analysis and trend prediction, AI is not merely a tool but a co-creator in the production and execution of impactful video marketing strategies.

One of the most exciting aspects of using AI in this sphere is its proficiency in targeted advertising, particularly on social media platforms. By leveraging advanced algorithms, marketers can now identify and reach precise audience segments like never before—making every dollar and pixel count.

So why should you invest your time in understanding this transformative synergy between AI and video marketing? Because it's not just the future of digital marketing—it's already shaping our present. And this book will serve as your comprehensive guide to navigating this dynamic terrain, from the essentials of video creation to the intricacies of personalised engagement, ethical considerations, and beyond.

Chapter 1: Overview

In a digital world overflowing with content, Video Marketing with AI has emerged as a game-changer. It's a potent blend of artificial intelligence and video technology, enabling businesses to connect and engage with audiences more effectively than ever before. Often heralded as a high-ROI investment, video marketing can be both technically challenging and time-consuming. This is where AI's capabilities come to the fore, making the process of creating, distributing, and optimising videos not just efficient but highly personalised and effective.

Such advancements empower brands to establish deeper and more meaningful connections with their target audiences. In the dog-eat-dog world of digital marketing, where gaining an edge over competitors is increasingly difficult, the AI-boosted video marketing strategy has proven to be indispensable.

AI in video marketing signifies the incorporation of artificial intelligence algorithms and technologies into every aspect of video production, distribution, and optimisation. The amalgamation of these two potent tools has radically elevated the effectiveness of video marketing campaigns. In fact, approximately 81% of businesses have already adopted video marketing, making it a linchpin in modern marketing strategy.

Crafting Compelling Video Titles with AI

The title of your video serves as the gateway to your brand's story. To convert viewers into customers, your title must serve dual purposes:

1. Clearly articulate the video's subject matter.

2. Be optimised for search engine algorithms (SEO).

Besides focusing on high-quality content, ensuring that your video's metadata—titles, descriptions, and subtitles—is SEO-friendly is crucial. AI-powered tools can assist in automatically generating SEO-rich subtitles and descriptions, boosting your video's online visibility.

Elevating Video Quality with AI

Content is king, but the way it is presented can make or break your video's impact. Poor production quality, such as unclear audio or shaky camera work, can adversely affect your brand's image. With AI, you can enhance these elements to produce a video that not only conveys your message effectively but also maintains high production standards.

Mastering the Art of Suspense

Engagement is not just about presenting everything upfront. To keep the viewer hooked, consider:

1. Creating suspense through teaser videos.

2. Crafting titles in the form of questions.

3. Encouraging viewer interaction through comments and questions.

4. Strategically withholding some information to spark curiosity.

Optimising Video Length with AI

AI tools can help you gauge the optimal length for your video content, ensuring you provide only the most crucial information while leaving some details to the audience's imagination. This prevents information overload and enhances viewer engagement.

The Importance of AI in the Current Video Landscape

The digital world is teeming with video content, making it challenging to stand out. AI brings a myriad of benefits to the table, such as:

- **Predictive Analytics:** AI's predictive abilities are game-changing. They can forecast emerging trends in video content, helping businesses to anticipate rather than react.

- **Hyper-Personalisation:** AI algorithms use viewer data to personalise content delivery, thereby increasing engagement and conversion rates significantly.

Real-world Applications

- **YouTube's Suggestion Algorithm:** YouTube uses AI to provide personalised video suggestions based on user activity, which keeps viewers engaged for longer periods.

- **Brands and AI:** Several forward-thinking brands have harnessed AI to analyse viewer reactions to their ads, using the insights gained to refine their marketing strategies.

- **TikTok's Personalized Feed:** TikTok's colossal success is thanks to AI-driven customization of user feeds. The algorithm watches how users interact with videos— what they like, share, or skip—and adjusts the content feed to match their preferences.

Benefits of AI in Video Marketing

- **Efficiency in Production:** AI helps in streamlining video content production, making it more cost-effective and efficient.

- **Enhanced Personalisation:** AI enables an unprecedented level of customisation, increasing viewer engagement and conversion rates.

- **Wider Reach:** Platforms like YouTube provide an extensive audience base, and AI can help you tap into this potential effectively.

- **Real-Time Feedback:** AI can facilitate real-time analytics and feedback, allowing for prompt adjustments to your marketing strategy.

AI's role in video marketing isn't merely evolutionary; it's revolutionary. By leveraging AI technologies in various aspects of video production and marketing, companies are making substantial strides in connecting with broader audiences and converting views into measurable business outcomes.

Chapter 2: Making & Editing Videos With AI – The Basics

In this chapter, we delve into the intricacies of video production, an area that has traditionally been a bottleneck for many aspiring marketers and small businesses. The conventional methods often require expensive equipment, a team of experts in videography, and an extensive post-production process. These hurdles often discourage individuals and small businesses from tapping into the immense potential of video marketing.

However, the advent of AI has revolutionised this domain. AI-enabled cameras, automated storyboarding, and intelligent editing tools have simplified video production to a point where virtually anyone can produce high-quality videos.

This chapter aims to guide you through the AI technologies that are breaking down the barriers in video production, making it more accessible and democratised than ever before.

In an age where the realms of technology and creativity are constantly intertwining, the burgeoning field of digital content creation has found a groundbreaking ally in Artificial Intelligence (AI). A novel paradigm, Making and Editing Videos with AI, is steadily crystallising as a transformative movement within the broader landscape of video production. This phenomenon has evolved to become more than a mere tool; it serves as a fulcrum around which a new age of creative video content orbits. Utilising the computational prowess and intelligence capabilities of AI, this paradigm shift promises to make video production more accessible, streamlined, and replete with limitless creative possibilities.

This comprehensive exploration aims to unpack the nuances of how AI serves as a disruptive force in video creation and editing. Whether you are a seasoned videographer or a beginner intrigued by the possibilities of video creation, this treatise will guide you through the expansive vistas that AI opens up in this field.

2.1 Video Creation with AI: Scripting, Storyboarding, and Shooting

In the fast-paced landscape of digital media, artificial intelligence is a breakthrough that has remarkably influenced every facet of video production. This technology serves as a linchpin, transforming the traditionally laborious stages of scripting, storyboarding, and shooting into a streamlined, efficient process. Whether you are a veteran in the field or a newcomer aiming to make your mark, this section aims to delve deeper into how AI is revolutionising these critical phases.

The AI Scriptwriter: Beyond Words to Wisdom

Gone are the days when scriptwriters had to solely rely on their intuition and creativity. Today's AI Scriptwriters employ advanced algorithms that wade through an ocean of data, be it prior successful scripts, trending topics, or viewer demographics, to generate script content tailored for a myriad of applications. Whether it's crafting catchy phrases for a social media marketing campaign, developing an engaging dialogue for an educational video, or spinning a compelling narrative for a feature film, AI has got it covered.

Advantages of AI Scriptwriting

Generating Outlines and Concepts: Conceptualising a unique and intriguing idea often represents one of the most formidable hurdles in scriptwriting. In this regard, AI platforms, like GPT-4, serve as a catalyst for creative thought. For instance, if you are stuck in a rut, a prompt such as "Write a dialogue between a detective and a time-travelling villain" could spawn an array of captivating plot points for a sci-fi thriller.

Enhancing Character Development: Crafting compelling characters is not just about slapping together a name and a role; it's about giving them depth, emotional resonance, and complexity. AI tools can dissect a character's proposed personality traits, historical background, and even ethical dilemmas, providing a writer with a multi-dimensional perspective. Imagine creating a character whose motivations change based on real-world events; AI can analyse current affairs to make your characters more relatable and up-to-date.

Storyboarding with AI: The Visual Alchemy

Storyboarding is akin to laying the foundation for a building. A well-constructed storyboard sets the stage for a successful video, and AI has proven to be an invaluable aid in this arena. Unlike traditional methods that relied on manual drawings and exhaustive revisions, AI can interpret the nuances and subtleties in a script to automatically render frame-by-frame visualisations.

Advantages of AI Storyboarding

Accelerated Workflow: Manually sketching out each scene can be an arduous task that consumes both time and resources. AI-empowered storyboarding systems can analyse a script within minutes, churning out detailed visual assets that a creative team can immediately act upon. For example, if a script specifies a dramatic sunset behind two characters, the AI can suggest optimal colour palettes, camera angles, and even potential locations.

Enhanced Team Collaboration: In traditional settings, misinterpretation of storyboards often led to costly delays and disagreements. AI-generated storyboards act as a universal visual language, eradicating ambiguities and fostering cohesive team collaborations. Whether you are a director with a grand vision or a designer focusing on the minutiae, everyone can align their objectives more cohesively.

AI-Powered Shooting: Capturing Perfection

As the world of AI has evolved, so too has its applicability in the actual shooting phase of video production. With functionalities ranging from optimal camera setting adjustments and facial recognition capabilities to dynamic camera movements, AI technology now plays a key role on set.

Advantages of AI-Powered Shooting

Superior Image Quality: Advanced AI algorithms can analyse individual frames in real-time, tweaking parameters like sharpness, contrast, and colour balance to create a visually stunning final product. Suppose you are shooting a fashion commercial; AI can detect the fabrics and colours, adjusting the lighting to make them pop and stay true to the brand's aesthetic.

Streamlined Workflow: The post-shooting phase often entails wading through heaps of visual content to identify usable footage. AI simplifies this process dramatically by tagging and cataloguing shots based on themes, characters, or even emotional tone. This not only saves time but also allows for a more organised, efficient editing process down the line.

The integration of AI in video production marks a quantum leap in how we approach the art of visual storytelling. From the embryonic stage of scriptwriting through the meticulous planning in storyboarding to the actual execution in shooting, AI serves as a groundbreaking tool that augments human creativity, optimises workflow, and elevates the end product to unparalleled heights. With these advancements, the future of video production promises to be more exciting, efficient, and limitless than ever before.

2.2 AI Video Editing Techniques and Tools

Once the shooting phase concludes, the video enters its next transformative phase: editing. This is where the raw footage is sculpted into a narrative, informational video, or any other end product. The advent of artificial intelligence in video editing has generated a paradigm shift, making the editing process not only more efficient but also innovative in ways previously unimaginable. Let's delve into some leading tools and techniques that harness the power of AI to offer a new dimension in video editing.

Descript: Transcription-First Approach

Descript is a trailblazing tool that alters the video editing landscape by putting transcription at its core. Gone are the days when editors needed to scrub through hours of footage; Descript provides a transcription almost instantaneously once the video is uploaded.

How it Works: Imagine you've recorded an hour-long interview. After uploading the video to Descript, you'll receive a text document that aligns with the audio. Now, editing the video is as simple as editing that document. Delete a sentence from the transcript, and the corresponding section of the video is also removed.

Advantages:

- **Efficiency:** You can edit long videos in a fraction of the time it would take using traditional methods.

- **Precision:** Fine-tuning is remarkably easier when you can see the spoken content in textual form.

Adobe Premiere Pro: The Blend of Tradition and Innovation

Adobe Premiere Pro has been an industry titan for years and has adroitly integrated AI functionalities without ditching its traditional video editing layout.

How it Works: Let's say you are working on a nature documentary. Adobe's Sensei AI can identify various elements in the footage like animals, plants, and weather conditions, making it easier to categorize and assemble sequences.

Advantages:

- **Advanced Features:** It combines the best of manual adjustments with AI automation, like automated colour correction.

- **Customisation:** It allows for extensive customisation, making it suitable for professionals who demand nuanced control over their edits.

Deepbrain AI: Bypassing Traditional Video Production

Deepbrain AI offers an entirely different avenue for video creation. It utilises AI-generated avatars and combines them with pre-recorded voiceovers in over 80 languages, effectively eliminating the need for human subjects and even shooting equipment.

How it Works: Imagine you're an educational content creator looking to produce a chemistry tutorial. With Deepbrain, you could select an AI-generated avatar as your "lecturer," upload a scripted voiceover, and have the avatar execute the tutorial flawlessly.

Advantages:

- **Resource Efficiency:** This tool is particularly valuable for small creators who don't have access to extensive resources.

- **Language Flexibility:** The ability to offer content in multiple languages widens your potential audience exponentially.

Vrew: Intuitive Text-Based Editing

Vrew is another revolutionary tool that simplifies video editing by aligning it closely with text editing. Like Descript, it converts video content into transcribed text, allowing you to cut, move, or delete sections of video via text manipulation.

How it Works: If you have a cooking video with multiple steps and realise that you forgot to include the baking stage, you can simply find the corresponding text and delete or replace it, effectively editing the video in sync.

Advantages:

- **Intuitive Workflow:** For those familiar with text editing but new to video editing, Vrew offers an easy learning curve.

- **Edit Accuracy:** Since you can see what's being said, the chances of making an error during the editing process are significantly reduced.

The integration of AI into video editing is nothing short of revolutionary. With a range of tools designed for various needs and preferences—from those who want to stay rooted in traditional methods to those looking to break away entirely—AI makes video editing faster, easier, and more innovative. These advancements signal a new era in video production, where creativity is only limited by one's imagination, not by the capabilities of their tools.

2.3 How AI Enhances Video Creation

Artificial Intelligence (AI) has advanced from being a supplementary tool to a formidable ally in video creation. It offers capabilities that transcend routine tasks, enriching the creative process and output. From facial recognition to automated editing and beyond, AI brings layers of sophistication, speed, and intelligence to the industry. Here, we'll explore these facets in detail.

Facial Recognition: Crafting Multi-Dimensional Narratives

AI-powered facial recognition technology is a game-changer, particularly in projects that require tracking individual characters or subjects throughout a video.

How it Works: Imagine a documentary focusing on a day in the life of a bustling city market. Facial recognition can follow specific vendors, capturing their activities, interactions, and even facial expressions, thereby providing a multi-dimensional narrative that enriches the storytelling.

Advantages:

- **Enhanced Storytelling:** The technology can help spotlight subtleties like changes in emotion, providing a more nuanced narrative.

- **Efficient Editing:** Knowing where a subject appears throughout the footage eliminates guesswork, making the editing process much more efficient.

Automated Video Editing: A Time-Saver and Quality Enhancer

AI algorithms have the power to automatically identify and assemble the most compelling sequences from hours of footage.

How it Works: Suppose you're creating a promotional video for a new product launch. Automated editing can sift through multiple takes to identify those with the most enthusiasm, clarity, and impact, compiling them into a riveting final product.

Advantages:

- **Time Efficiency:** Manually identifying the best takes from hours of footage is a time-consuming process that AI can complete in a fraction of the time.

- **Quality Assurance:** Algorithms can be calibrated to focus on elements like lighting, composition, and emotional resonance, ensuring a top-quality final product.

Video Stabilisation: Smoothing Out the Edges

AI-based video stabilisation tools have revolutionised how we deal with shaky or inconsistent footage. These tools offer remarkable accuracy in stabilising videos.

How it Works: Picture filming a nature documentary in a moving boat. Traditional stabilisation might still leave you with shaky footage, but AI-based stabilisation can counteract the boat's motions, offering a smoother, more professional result.

Advantages:

- **Superior Quality:** Advanced algorithms can correct even the most erratic of movements, from hand tremors to vehicular bumps.

- **Flexible Application:** These tools can be applied in post-production or, in some cases, during the actual filming through AI-enabled cameras.

Object and Scene Recognition: The Smart Cutter

Scene and object recognition technologies can automatically identify key moments, whether they are critical plays in a sports match or climactic scenes in a drama.

How it Works: Consider a football match where multiple noteworthy events occur. AI can automatically recognise the moments of goals, fouls, and other high-impact plays, flagging them for inclusion in the final edit.

Advantages:

- **Smart Editing:** AI ensures that key moments are not overlooked, streamlining the editing process.

- **Narrative Enhancement:** By focusing on high-impact scenes, AI aids in constructing a compelling storyline or highlight reel.

AI as a Creative Partner

AI serves as more than just a tool; it's an evolving creative partner. Its capabilities extend beyond mere functionality, transforming the very essence of how videos are conceptualised, produced, and edited. As AI continues to evolve, it is not just setting new technical standards but is also expanding the boundaries of creativity in digital content creation.

Chapter 3: Content Analysis

In this chapter, we delve into the intricacies of audience targeting, a crucial yet often daunting aspect of video marketing.

Traditionally, effective targeting required marketers to sift through copious amounts of data, conduct extensive market research, and still often rely on educated guesses. This was a tedious, time-consuming process that often erected barriers for small businesses and individual marketers.

However, AI has emerged as a game-changer in this space. Advanced algorithms can now analyse big data in real-time, automating the process of audience segmentation and allowing for incredibly precise targeting strategies.

Even those with a modest budget or limited expertise can utilise AI tools to engage with the most relevant audience segments, thereby democratising the otherwise complex world of audience targeting.

Video analytics has been a foundational element in the realms of security and customer service for several years. The technology has been pivotal in safeguarding premises, tracking intruders, and analysing customer footfall in retail spaces, among other applications. However, with the advent of Artificial Intelligence (AI), the field of video analytics is undergoing a transformative shift, bringing a level of sophistication and capability that was previously unimaginable.

Traditionally, video analytics mainly involved capturing and storing video footage for later review. Security personnel would pore over hours of footage to identify incidents or assess vulnerabilities, often manually. In customer service applications, businesses would collect video evidence to understand customer movement patterns within a retail space or monitor staff performance. While useful, these applications have limitations in real-time decision-making and predictive analysis.

Enter Artificial Intelligence, a groundbreaking technology that has accelerated our capabilities across diverse fields, from healthcare to autonomous vehicles. In the realm of video analytics, AI has the ability to process and analyse live streams of video data in real-time. The implications of this are enormous. For example, an AI-driven video surveillance system in a shopping centre could not only detect unusual movements that deviate from normative behavioural patterns (such as someone loitering around a closed shop late at night) but also predict potential security incidents before they happen by analysing trends in movement, facial recognition, and even biometric indicators like heart rate, which some advanced systems can pick up.

In terms of staffing, AI-powered video analytics can determine when more staff are needed in certain areas of a store or venue based on real-time customer movements. For instance, if sensors pick up unusually high footfall near a promotional display in a supermarket, the system could alert management to deploy more staff to that area for crowd control and better customer service.

Customer behaviour is another area where AI-driven video analytics can provide unprecedented insights. Beyond just tracking movement, these systems can analyse facial expressions to gauge customer reactions to store displays or products. This kind of emotional analytics could offer retailers a deeper understanding of customer preferences and tailor their strategies accordingly. Imagine a retail clothing store where AI identifies that customers frequently frown at a particular display; this could prompt an immediate reassessment of the products being offered or how they are presented.

But AI's application in video analytics is not limited to the worlds of security and customer service. Its impact resonates through the broader, rapidly evolving landscape of multimedia content. Whether it's deciphering complex scenes in vast libraries of video archives, transcribing and translating global news coverage in real-time, or even influencing the creative processes in filmmaking through data-driven insights, AI is radically changing our approach to video and audio content.

This chapter aims to explore these and many other groundbreaking applications of AI in video analytics. We will delve deep into the role AI plays in decoding complex video and audio data, look at its transformative impact on various industries including entertainment, and discuss its increasingly vital role in enhancing audience engagement across platforms.

3.1: Role of AI in Analysing Video Content and Audio

In today's digital landscape saturated with multimedia content, the ability to efficiently analyse video and audio data is indispensable. Artificial Intelligence (AI) has emerged as a revolutionary tool, fundamentally altering how we approach, comprehend, and engage with multimedia. From refining video editing processes to personalising viewer experiences, AI offers a plethora of applications. Here, we will dive deeper into the various roles AI plays in analysing video and audio content.

Improving Video Editing Efficiency

Traditional video editing is a painstaking process, often requiring hours of manual review to identify the most relevant clips. AI has significantly streamlined this workflow. For instance, in a busy newsroom where meeting deadlines is paramount, AI can quickly scan through hours of footage to find clips relevant to a breaking story.

- **Content Analysis**: By using deep learning algorithms, AI can understand the central theme of various scenes, thereby eliminating irrelevant footage. For example, if you're creating a documentary on climate change, the system could automatically filter out scenes that are not directly related to the topic.

- **Facial Recognition**: AI can track key characters throughout a video, helping maintain a coherent narrative. In political coverage, for example, facial recognition can focus on the speaker, ignoring irrelevant crowd shots or background activity.

- **Scene Segmentation**: The technology can also break down a lengthy video into logical sequences, aiding in the editing process. This is particularly useful in long interviews or panel discussions, where it's essential to categorise content by topic or speaker for easy navigation.

Real-time Transcription and Translation

One of AI's remarkable capabilities is its speed and accuracy in transcribing spoken language to text, and subsequently translating it into different languages.

- **ASR Technology**: Automatic Speech Recognition (ASR) can quickly and accurately transcribe interviews or debates. Imagine a high-profile international summit; ASR technology could live-transcribe speeches, aiding journalists and policymakers in real-time.

- **Multi-language Support**: The technology can translate the transcribed text into 80+ languages almost instantaneously, enabling global accessibility. This is vital for breaking news events, ensuring that information is universally disseminated.

Personalised Content Recommendations

In an era of information overload, AI helps viewers find content that aligns with their interests, thereby boosting engagement and satisfaction.

- **User Profiling**: AI creates detailed user profiles based on factors like viewing history, search queries, and even the amount of time spent watching specific content. For example, if a user frequently watches documentaries on a streaming platform, AI will likely recommend more of the same genre.

- **Dynamic Suggestions**: As a user continues to engage with a platform, the AI system adapts and refines its recommendations, making them increasingly personalised over time.

Enhancing Audio Quality

Maintaining high audio quality is crucial, especially in today's remote working environment where clarity in communication can make or break a deal.

- **Noise Cancellation**: AI can identify and separate background noise, such as the clattering of dishes in a café or the hum of an air conditioner, to deliver crystal-clear voice output.
- **Audio Restoration**: For older, degraded audio files, AI can recover and restore them to their original quality, making it invaluable for archivists and historians.

Creative Applications in Entertainment

AI is beginning to leave its mark on the creative facets of the entertainment industry, offering data-driven insights that can influence storytelling.

- **Storyline Analysis**: Through Natural Language Processing (NLP), AI can evaluate the strength of a plot, the depth of character development, and other narrative elements. This could be a tool for scriptwriters to refine their stories before they even hit the pre-production stage.
- **Sentiment Analysis**: By gauging audience reactions to existing works—such as reviews or social media mentions—AI can predict the potential success of new projects.

Improving Accessibility

AI's power isn't just reserved for large corporations or media conglomerates. Thanks to user-friendly interfaces and pre-built models, even small businesses can harness the potential of AI-powered analytics.

- **User-friendly Interfaces**: Many AI tools come with intuitive dashboards that require little to no prior experience in machine learning, lowering the entry barriers to advanced analytics.
- **Pre-built Models**: These offer a range of templates tailored for various industries, from retail to healthcare, allowing businesses to tap into consumer behaviour data without the need for specialized expertise.

By deeply integrating AI into the analysis of video and audio content, we are witnessing a paradigm shift in multimedia management, one that promises to make our interaction with this content more enriching, engaging, and efficient than ever before.

3.2: Analysis and Audience Engagement with AI

In the current digital landscape, the line between consumer and content has become increasingly blurred, making audience engagement a pivotal part of any business strategy. Artificial Intelligence (AI) serves as a critical tool in this dynamic ecosystem, offering a myriad of benefits that extend from enhancing user experience to shaping advertising strategies. Let's dive into the specifics.

Personalised Content Recommendations

AI-driven personalisation is a compelling feature that not only retains user attention but also creates value for businesses and advertisers. For instance, platforms like Netflix employ AI to recommend movies based on users' previous viewing history, ensuring that their platform becomes a go-to source for entertainment. But this isn't solely for the benefit of the viewer; it also allows advertisers to target users more precisely.

- **Example**: A user who frequently listens to jazz playlists on Spotify might start receiving adverts for upcoming jazz concerts or instrument shops, making advertising more relevant and less intrusive.

Targeted Advertising Using AI

AI algorithms dissect extensive datasets comprising user behaviour, preferences, and past engagements to craft individualised advertising campaigns.

- **Example**: If a user often shops for sportswear online, an e-commerce website could display adverts for the latest running shoes or gym equipment. These custom ads have been demonstrated to convert passive viewers into active buyers, enhancing return on investment (ROI).

Enhanced Customer Insights

Data analytics powered by AI offer businesses granular insights into consumer behaviour, which can inform decisions across different verticals, from marketing to product development.

- **Example**: A streaming platform may observe that dramas are more frequently watched during weekdays while comedies are popular over weekends. This data can influence content acquisition and scheduling decisions.

AI-Powered Chatbots for Customer Engagement

AI chatbots are revolutionising customer service. They can answer queries, solve problems, and even upsell products, all while collecting data to further personalise user interactions.

- **Example**: A chatbot on a travel website could recommend holiday packages based on a user's past travel history and preferences, turning a casual query into a potential sale.

Challenges of Using AI for Audience Reach and Engagement

While AI offers significant advantages, it also brings forth a set of challenges that need to be addressed responsibly.

- **Data Privacy and Security Concerns**: Compliance with data protection laws like GDPR is non-negotiable. Data breaches could lead to legal repercussions and erode customer trust.

- **Lack of Trust and Ethical Considerations**: The role of AI in society is still viewed with scepticism by some. The misuse of AI for nefarious purposes, such as facial recognition in unwarranted surveillance, raises ethical concerns.

- **Investment and Expertise**: The initial cost of implementing AI solutions can be daunting, especially for small to medium enterprises. Beyond the technology, businesses also need to invest in skilled professionals who can manage these complex systems.

- **Lack of Transparency**: AI algorithms can sometimes seem like "black boxes," leading to issues of trust. Businesses need to prioritise algorithmic transparency to explain how data is used and how decisions are made.

The infusion of AI into the realms of video analytics and audience engagement is nothing short of transformative. It offers an amalgamation of opportunities that impact various sectors, including entertainment, retail, and beyond. However, this potential comes bundled with ethical and financial considerations that businesses must thoughtfully address. By balancing the benefits with the inherent challenges, we can harness AI's full potential to redefine how we interact with content and, by extension, with the world.

Chapter 4: The Transformative Role of AI in Personalising Customer Experiences

In this chapter, we delve into the intricacies of video analytics and customer engagement—two pivotal aspects of video marketing that have traditionally posed significant challenges for marketers. Before the advent of AI, businesses often relied on rudimentary metrics like views and likes, which provided only a surface-level understanding of audience interaction.

This lack of nuanced insight made it difficult for small businesses or newcomers to compete with larger companies, which could afford sophisticated analytics tools and teams of data scientists. With the rise of AI technologies, this landscape is dramatically changing.

Now, even small businesses can leverage advanced analytics to gain in-depth knowledge about viewer behaviour, preferences, and engagement levels. AI tools democratise the analytics field by making it accessible and understandable, effectively lowering the barriers to entry for everyone.

The dynamics of brand-customer relationships have undergone a monumental transformation with the advent of Artificial Intelligence (AI). Prior to AI, the scope for personalisation in consumer engagement was limited to rudimentary strategies like sending emails addressed with the customer's first name or recommending products based on basic consumer profiling. Fast-forward to the AI era, and personalisation has advanced to become a complex, data-driven, real-time interaction that significantly influences various facets of businesses, consumers, and even society at large. Below, we delve into these dimensions in detail.

One of the primary ways AI elevates customer engagement is through real-time personalisation. For instance, consider an online shopping platform that uses AI algorithms to analyse your past purchases, viewed items, and even time spent hovering over products. Leveraging this data, the platform can dynamically tailor its homepage to display products or offers that are most relevant to you. Amazon is an epitome of this strategy, which leads to substantially higher engagement rates, and consequently, higher sales. A customer who feels 'seen' by a brand is more likely to engage positively, reaffirming the brand's decision to invest in AI technologies.

Personalisation isn't just about presenting what's relevant; it's also about eliminating what's not. For example, streaming services like Netflix or Spotify eliminate the noise of irrelevant choices, curating personalised playlists or series suggestions. In doing so, these services foster a sense of consumer loyalty because they consistently deliver value that aligns closely with individual preferences. Over time, this loyalty can translate into increased sales and stronger consumer-brand relationships. For instance, a Spotify user may decide to transition from the free tier to a premium subscription, seeing the tangible benefits of an ad-free, personalised experience.

The rise of AI in personalisation also prompts a major shift in business models and marketing strategies. Brands now allocate more resources towards data analytics, behavioural profiling, and AI-driven automated systems, redefining roles within the marketing departments. Traditional methods of mass advertising are giving way to targeted ad campaigns based on intricate data models. Take the example of Coca-Cola, which used AI to analyse social media trends and customer feedback to create a new product, Cherry Sprite, within a short span of time. This kind of agility in responding to consumer demands is unprecedented and rewrites the rulebook on product development and market entry strategies.

As consumers become accustomed to highly personalised experiences, their expectations shift, raising the bar for all brands. No longer satisfied with generic experiences, the modern consumer demands more—be it in product choices, content, or customer service. Even the hospitality industry is jumping on the bandwagon, with hotels like Marriott using AI to offer personalised travel experiences, right from the room ambiance down to the type of toiletries provided.

As AI becomes the new normal, it starts to impact societal norms and expectations. The efficiency and convenience offered by AI may raise questions about data privacy and ethics. The Cambridge Analytica scandal serves as a cautionary tale, highlighting the potential misuse of personal data for targeted political advertising.

Despite the manifold advantages, AI's ability to amass and analyse colossal volumes of personal data does raise ethical dilemmas. Questions arise about who owns this data, how securely it's stored, and how transparently it's used. Legislative measures like GDPR in the European Union are stepping stones towards a more controlled use of personal data, but the conversation around ethical AI is ongoing and complex.

AI's integration into brand-customer relationships is multi-faceted, replete with both remarkable opportunities and inherent challenges. As we continue to unlock AI's potential for creating deeply personalised experiences, it becomes increasingly imperative to navigate the ethical landscape responsibly. Brands must strike a balance between offering hyper-personalisation and safeguarding consumer privacy, all while adapting to rapidly evolving technologies and consumer expectations.

In today's digital age, where attention spans are dwindling and information overload is the norm, a personalised digital experience has moved from being a luxury to a necessity. Imagine scrolling through your social media feed and encountering only videos that resonate with your specific interests—whether it's travel, cooking, or technology. AI is the driving force behind this transformation, utilising recommendation algorithms, chatbots, and predictive analytics to take content creation, specifically video content, to new heights. Companies like YouTube and Netflix already employ complex algorithms to ensure you see content that is directly aligned with your viewing history.

Defining Personalised Video Content

Personalised video content takes marketing personalisation to a nuanced level. This is not just about inserting a user's name into a video but curating content based on a plethora of data points—from viewing history to location to social media activity. Take, for instance, the "Year in Review" videos that platforms like Facebook or Spotify create. These videos encapsulate your interactions and preferences over the past year, presenting them in a unique, visual format that feels personal and engaging.

According to a study by Twilio, such tailored experiences are so effective that 49% of customers are likely to become repeat buyers. Furthermore, a third of consumers would opt for a brand they're familiar with over cheaper or more convenient alternatives, provided they've had a positive personalised experience.

Advantages of Personalised Video Content

For Users:

1. **Improved User Experience**: Personalised video content makes users feel valued and understood, which cultivates a positive user experience. This enhances the overall relationship between the brand and the user. For example, a fitness app could generate custom workout videos based on a user's past activities, goals, and preferences, making the user more likely to engage regularly with the app.

2. **Enhanced Relevance**: With AI's data-crunching capabilities, the videos that are presented to users are closely aligned with their individual preferences. This eliminates the 'noise' of irrelevant content, making the user's online experience far more enjoyable and efficient. Think about a foodie who only gets cooking and restaurant review videos in their feed, sparing them from unrelated content like political debates or celebrity gossip.

3. **Increased Engagement**: By serving content that resonates with users, there's a greater chance they will engage with it by liking, sharing, or commenting. This, in turn, amplifies the reach and effectiveness of the content. For instance, a personalised how-to video about gardening will likely be shared within communities interested in gardening, thereby exponentially increasing its reach.

For Businesses:

1. **Customer Retention**: When a brand consistently provides content that resonates with a user, it fosters a sense of loyalty, turning occasional users into long-term customers. A movie streaming service that continuously offers films and series in line with a user's tastes will likely retain that customer for years to come.

2. **Higher Conversion Rates**: Well-tailored content not only engages users but also prompts them to take desired actions, like making a purchase or signing up for a newsletter. For example, a personalised video from an online retailer, highlighting items related to what the user has previously browsed or purchased, can nudge the user towards making another purchase.

Personalised AI video content has become a linchpin in modern digital marketing strategies for both enhancing user experience and driving business outcomes. As the technology continues to evolve, personalisation is expected to become even more refined, setting new standards for what users expect from their digital experiences. It's not just about serving content anymore; it's about serving the *right* content. This level of precision not only benefits the consumer but also gives businesses a distinct competitive edge, making the investment in AI-driven personalised video content a win-win for all parties involved.

4.2 Techniques for Creating Compelling, Personalised Videos

Utilising Customer Data

The first step in crafting a compelling personalised video lies in understanding who your audience is and what they are interested in. With AI-driven analytics, brands can segment their customer base using parameters such as age, geographical location, online behaviour, and past purchases. These data points serve as the foundation for creating highly targeted video content.

For example, a travel company could produce region-specific videos based on the geographical location of the audience. A UK-based audience might receive personalised video suggestions on weekend getaways in the Lake District or cultural experiences in London, while a US-based audience could get videos about road trips in the American Southwest or food tours in New York City. The data ensures that the content is not just engaging but also incredibly relevant, which is likely to increase user interaction and drive conversions.

Customer Testimonials

In an age where customers trust peer reviews as much as personal recommendations, video testimonials serve as highly potent tools for building brand credibility. These are not merely videos of satisfied customers; they can be smartly integrated into a personalised content strategy. Imagine a software-as-a-service (SaaS) company using AI to recommend testimonial videos that relate specifically to the features a prospective customer has shown interest in.

For instance, if you've been exploring project management features on a SaaS platform, a testimonial video discussing those specific capabilities will automatically hold more weight and encourage trust. Not only does this validate the brand, but it also resonates with the potential customer's specific needs and queries, making the video content extremely effective.

Creative Approaches

While data and testimonials provide a strong backbone for personalised video content, creativity is the element that truly differentiates a brand. Utilising unique storytelling techniques, integrating Augmented Reality (AR) experiences, or even creating a catchy jingle can elevate your brand's video content from informative to unforgettable.

Consider a furniture brand that uses AR to allow users to virtually 'place' furniture items in their homes through a video. This interactive video experience not only showcases the product but also makes the user part of the story, thereby creating a memorable brand experience.

Another example could be a sustainable fashion brand crafting a jingle that highlights its eco-friendly initiatives. This jingle can be used in personalised video content targeted at eco-conscious customers, resonating deeply with their values and making the brand more memorable.

AI has a multi-faceted role in the production of personalised videos. From using detailed customer data for targeted messaging to reinforcing brand value with curated testimonials, and from setting a brand apart with inventive creative approaches, AI enables brands to reach their audience like never before. The end result is not just high user engagement but also a deeper emotional connection between the brand and the consumer. As technology evolves, the possibilities for personalisation in video content are virtually endless, making it a critical aspect of any modern marketing strategy.

4.3 Challenges and Pitfalls of Personalised Video Marketing

Time Constraints

The implementation of AI in personalised video marketing is not an instantaneous process; it requires a significant time investment. From the conceptualisation of content ideas to data gathering, from production to post-production activities—each step needs meticulous planning and execution. Collaboration among marketing, data analysis, and creative departments is crucial, but this can be time-consuming and can sometimes slow down the go-to-market strategy.

For example, a health and wellness brand might want to produce personalised video content focusing on different types of fitness routines tailored to various age groups. The planning alone would involve data analytics to identify target age groups, the creative team to storyboard each video, and the production team for filming and editing. Then there's the task of integrating these videos into a personalised marketing strategy, which would need more time for testing and implementation.

Content Ideas

Even with AI tools at their disposal, marketers still face the challenge of generating fresh, relevant, and compelling content. According to various studies, almost 30% of marketers cite this as a significant hurdle. While AI can offer suggestions based on consumer behaviour, predictive analytics, and market trends, these are only as good as the creativity that utilises them.

Take, for instance, a home goods retailer that's run multiple successful campaigns around seasonal home decoration. The data might indicate that these campaigns were highly engaging, tempting the brand to repeat similar campaigns. But audiences could easily grow fatigued with repetitive content, and the challenge here lies in leveraging data to create fresh yet relevant video content.

AI can help overcome this creative block by offering insights into what type of content consumers are currently engaging with outside of your brand. If the data shows a surge in interest in sustainable living, for example, the home goods retailer might consider producing a new line of eco-friendly products and accompanying that launch with personalised video content.

Additional Pitfalls to Consider

1. **Data Privacy Concerns**: As personalised video marketing becomes increasingly data-driven, it's imperative to consider privacy regulations, such as GDPR in the European Union or the Data Protection Act in the UK. Failure to comply can not only result in hefty fines but also damage to brand reputation.

2. **Algorithmic Bias**: AI is only as unbiased as the data it's trained on. If the data set is skewed, the resulting personalised content could unintentionally alienate portions of the audience. Brands need to constantly review and update their AI algorithms to ensure inclusivity.

3. **User Skepticism**: As AI-driven personalisation becomes more sophisticated, there's a potential for users to find it 'creepy' or invasive, defeating the entire purpose of creating a personalised experience.

While AI offers revolutionary tools for crafting deeply personalised and effective video marketing campaigns, brands must be cognisant of the challenges and pitfalls that come with it. Time constraints and idea generation are just the tip of the iceberg. Ethical considerations around data privacy and algorithmic bias, as well as understanding and managing consumer perceptions, are crucial for a successful personalised video marketing strategy.

4.4 Legal and Ethical Concerns

In today's data-driven world, compliance with privacy regulations like GDPR (General Data Protection Regulation) in the EU or the Data Protection Act in the UK is not optional; it's mandatory. AI's capacity to collect and analyse large swaths of personal data brings this issue to the forefront. Brands must adopt stringent data governance practices to ensure they're only collecting data they need and are authorised to use, all while safeguarding it against breaches.

Example: A fashion e-commerce platform that uses AI to tailor video ads based on customer browsing history must explicitly inform customers that their data is being collected and used for this purpose. This could be implemented through a clear and concise pop-up message requiring customer consent before data is collected.

Ethical Standards

AI-driven personalised video content should not only be non-discriminatory but should also aim to be inclusive. Brands must monitor algorithms for any biases, whether they're related to age, gender, ethnicity, or any other demographic factors. Algorithmic fairness is not merely an ethical necessity but also a business imperative, as discriminatory content can severely damage a brand's reputation.

Example: A travel agency promoting a holiday package might unintentionally focus too much on one demographic in their personalised video marketing campaign. This could alienate other potential customers and can also draw ethical and legal concerns.

4.5 Resource Allocation and ROI

Balanced Marketing Strategy

While the benefits of AI-driven personalised video content are evident, it should not become the only focus of a brand's marketing strategy. Other channels, whether they are traditional advertising mediums like print and television or digital mediums like social media and email, also play crucial roles in customer engagement and should not be neglected.

Example: A tech company may find that their target demographic responds well to personalised video content but should also remember that professional networking sites like LinkedIn or industry events may be equally or more effective for B2B engagements.

Calculating ROI

Investment in AI technologies for video marketing can be considerable. The costs include not just the technology itself but also data analytics expertise, creative development, and ongoing management. Therefore, an in-depth ROI analysis is crucial to justify these expenses and fine-tune future strategies. Key performance indicators (KPIs) such as engagement rates, conversion rates, and customer lifetime value can offer insights into the effectiveness of a personalised video marketing campaign.

Example: An online grocery store employing AI-driven personalised video content should keep track of metrics like how many users made a purchase after watching a video, average order value, and customer retention rate. This data would be pivotal in determining the ROI and the long-term viability of the campaign.

4.6 Testing and Optimisation

The digital landscape is ever-changing, and what worked yesterday may not be effective today. This fluidity makes the continuous testing and optimisation of video marketing campaigns indispensable. While AI and data analytics provide robust initial insights for crafting personalised videos, the true measure of effectiveness comes from real-world performance metrics.

A/B Tests

One of the most direct methods to evaluate the effectiveness of different video marketing approaches is through A/B tests. This involves creating two or more versions of a video, each with a distinct element—perhaps a different call-to-action, background music, or video length—and then serving these to different subsets of your audience.

Example: A fitness brand could A/B test two versions of a video promoting a new exercise bike. One video might focus on the bike's technical features while the other centres on customer testimonials. By measuring metrics such as click-through rates and conversion rates, the brand can determine which approach resonates more with its audience.

Analytics Dashboards

Modern video hosting platforms offer comprehensive analytics dashboards that provide a wealth of data, including view counts, engagement rates, and viewer demographics. These dashboards are crucial for gauging the real-time impact of a video campaign and identifying areas for improvement.

Example: An online bookstore could use an analytics dashboard to see how long viewers are watching a promotional video for a new thriller novel. If the analytics indicate that viewers generally stop watching after 20 seconds, it might be worth revisiting the video's pacing or content to keep the audience engaged for a longer period.

Consumer Surveys

While quantitative data is valuable, it doesn't always tell the whole story. Consumer surveys can offer qualitative insights into viewer perception, which is particularly useful for understanding why certain metrics are performing the way they are.

Example: A travel agency might send out a survey asking viewers what they liked or disliked about a recently launched video on luxury holiday packages. Feedback like "The video was too long" or "I wanted to see more of the destination and less of people talking" can provide actionable insights for future content creation.

The true strength of AI in video marketing doesn't just lie in its ability to create highly personalised content, but also in its capacity to adapt and refine this content based on real-world data. Employing a mix of A/B testing, analytics dashboards, and consumer surveys not only enables a nuanced understanding of consumer behaviour but also allows for the iterative improvement of video marketing strategies. In a competitive digital environment, the brands that can adapt are the ones that will ultimately thrive.

Navigating the Complex Landscape of AI-Driven Video Marketing

Artificial Intelligence has undeniably become a linchpin in modern marketing, fundamentally altering how brands interact with their customers. With capabilities ranging from highly targeted recommendations to real-time personalisation, AI offers opportunities to create deeper, more meaningful connections. But while the allure of these technological advancements is strong, it's equally crucial to approach them with a tempered, ethical lens.

The Dual Edges of the AI Sword

The application of AI in marketing, particularly in the realm of video content, presents an array of benefits. For instance, tailored experiences resonate more with consumers, often resulting in increased loyalty and better conversion rates. However, it's imperative to remember that this powerful tool can be a double-edged sword. The same algorithms that can enhance user experience can also compromise privacy or perpetuate biases if not carefully managed.

Consider the case of a brand using AI algorithms to deliver personalised fitness tips through video content. While this is innovative and valuable, the brand must be cautious not to inadvertently breach data privacy norms or create content that could be perceived as discriminatory based on age, gender, or physical capabilities.

The Ethical and Practical Imperatives

Compliance with data protection regulations like GDPR, especially in an era where data is the new currency, can't be overstated. Brands not only need to secure explicit consent for data collection and usage but also ensure that their algorithms are transparent and non-discriminatory.

A skincare brand targeting their video ads might need to make sure they aren't excluding specific demographics unintentionally, which could be viewed as discriminatory. They must also offer clear ways for consumers to opt-out of data collection efforts, aligning with privacy laws.

A Balanced Approach to Investment and Strategy

While AI offers lucrative avenues for customer engagement and revenue generation, it should complement, not overshadow, other aspects of a brand's marketing strategy. A diversified approach ensures that a brand can adapt to shifting trends and consumer behaviours without being overly reliant on a single channel or technology.

Looking Ahead: An Ecosystem of Responsible Innovation

The evolving landscape of AI-powered video marketing is laden with both challenges and opportunities. However, by conscientiously navigating ethical considerations, dedicating resources wisely, and maintaining a continuous cycle of testing and optimisation, brands can not only make the most of AI's enormous potential but also build more trustworthy, engaging, and successful relationships with their customer base.

Chapter 5 - SEO and AI for Video Marketing

In traditional marketing landscapes, Search Engine Optimisation (SEO) for video content often presented a daunting challenge for many, especially small businesses and individual marketers.

The complexities of keyword research, metadata optimisation, and keeping up with ever-changing search engine algorithms made it difficult for those without specialised knowledge or resources to compete. But with the advent of AI, these barriers are beginning to crumble.

AI tools can automatically analyse user behaviour, suggest relevant keywords, and even optimise video metadata, leveling the playing field. What was once a specialised skill set is becoming more automated and accessible, allowing even newcomers to effectively optimise their video content for search engines.

This shift not only simplifies SEO complexities but also democratises access to high-ranking visibility, enabling anyone with the right tools to gain a competitive edge.

The interplay between Search Engine Optimisation (SEO) and Artificial Intelligence (AI) has monumental implications for video marketing. In an era where video consumption is at an all-time high, brands that capitalise on the symbiotic relationship between SEO and AI are well-positioned to dominate the online video landscape. Whether it's YouTube, Vimeo, or self-hosted videos on a brand's website, grasping the complexities of SEO and AI provides a significant competitive advantage. This chapter unpacks the intricate dynamics of tagging, descriptions, and algorithm optimisation, with a particular focus on how AI amplifies the power of these strategies.

5.1 Tagging, Descriptions, and Algorithm Optimisation

The Underestimated Value of Metadata

One of the most often disregarded aspects of SEO is metadata. This includes tags, titles, and descriptions that are pivotal for enhancing your video's discoverability. Tags act like markers, titles serve as headlines to captivate interest, and descriptions provide a summary to both viewers and search engines alike. Effective metadata not only makes your video more searchable but also significantly influences the click-through rate (CTR).

Consider the case of a cooking channel that focuses on quick and healthy meals. By consistently tagging its videos with relevant keywords such as 'quick dinner ideas,' '30-minute recipes,' or 'healthy meal plans,' the channel can drastically improve its visibility. Combine this tagging strategy with compelling titles like "Cook a Healthy Meal in 30 Minutes!" and thorough descriptions, and you're setting the stage for organic traffic growth and higher CTRs.

AI-Powered Algorithm Optimisation

Traditional SEO approaches have limitations in how effectively they adapt to continually evolving search engine algorithms. This is where AI steps in, serving as a catalyst for revolutionary improvements in how we approach SEO. Advanced AI algorithms can deeply analyse user interactions and behaviours, providing actionable insights to better tailor your content for search engine optimization.

Tools like MarketMuse or Clearscope use AI to evaluate high-ranking content and recommend not just tags but also content structures that can boost SEO. They can even suggest the optimal length for your video descriptions or indicate the best time to post your content based on when your audience is most active online.

Symbiosis: The Future of SEO and AI in Video Marketing

Search engines are continually evolving, with their algorithms incorporating increasingly sophisticated AI to deliver better search results. This makes it critical for brands to leverage their own AI capabilities to dissect and understand these algorithms effectively. A well-rounded understanding of search engine behaviour, enabled by AI analytics, can help businesses tailor their video content to meet both user needs and algorithmic preferences.

Example: Platforms like Google Analytics and Adobe Analytics have started incorporating AI elements to their tools, allowing for a more nuanced understanding of factors affecting your video rankings. By leveraging these analytics, brands can discern not just what kind of content gets ranked higher but also understand the types of videos that encourage longer watch times, thus fulfilling criteria that search algorithms often use to determine quality and relevance.

By capitalising on the synergistic relationship between SEO and AI, marketers can significantly bolster the reach, engagement, and overall success of their video content. This collaborative approach offers a multi-faceted strategy, effectively manoeuvring the complexities of the modern digital landscape.

5.2 Competitor Analysis with AI
Identifying Strengths and Weaknesses

One of the first steps in a robust marketing strategy is understanding the competitive landscape. Artificial Intelligence has revolutionised this aspect by offering more than just a superficial look at competitors' performance. AI dives deep to provide extensive insights, including keyword efficiency, user engagement metrics like views and likes, and even complex factors like emotional resonance of content.

Take a hypothetical scenario where a fitness brand is eager to outshine a competitor in the realm of video marketing. AI can come to the rescue by analysing not just typical metrics such as audience retention but also more nuanced variables. For instance, it could study the average time users are spending on specific workout routines and correlate this with sentiment analysis gathered from viewer comments. This can help the brand zero in on what types of content resonate most and where there might be room for innovation.

Predictive Analytics for Proactive Strategies

Competitor analysis has traditionally been about looking at past and current performances to gauge future possibilities. AI takes this to the next level by being predictive. Sophisticated algorithms can crunch current data to provide forecasts on future trends, giving your brand a potential first-mover advantage.

For example, if the AI analytics tools indicate that in the fitness industry, short-form workout videos are steadily outpacing long-form tutorials, this insight would allow you to pivot your strategy before your competitors catch on. Imagine the advantage of being the first to produce a series of impactful 5-minute workout clips right when the audience starts to lean towards shorter content.

Actionable Recommendations for Precise Adjustments

Perhaps the most powerful feature of AI-driven competitor analysis is the specificity of its recommendations. Unlike traditional methods that provide broad suggestions, AI can sift through large data sets to identify the exact elements that could push your video marketing strategy over the top.

The AI analytics could point out that videos with bright, text-rich thumbnails are receiving significantly higher click-through rates than those with image-only thumbnails. It might also identify that videos ending with a strong, clear call-to-action like "Subscribe Now for More Tips!" tend to retain audiences better. Incorporating these highly targeted elements can dramatically impact your video's effectiveness.

A Symbiotic Future of SEO and AI for Video Marketing

Integrating SEO and AI becomes a formidable strategy when it comes to enhancing the efficiency and reach of your video marketing campaigns. They work hand-in-hand to not only improve metadata optimisation and algorithmic comprehension but also to deliver deeply insightful competitor analysis.

The future isn't about choosing between SEO and AI; it's about leveraging these powerful technologies in unison to forge a path to unparalleled video marketing success. By doing so, brands can adapt more rapidly to market changes, make smarter strategic choices, and ultimately, build stronger connections with their audiences.

Chapter 6- How AI Picks Videos for You to Watch?
In the past, the task of video content curation was a significant challenge for marketers and content providers. They had to rely on rudimentary algorithms, manual curation, or the unpredictable whims of viral trends to get their content in front of viewers. This often resulted in a mismatch between viewer interests and the videos presented to them, leading to less engagement and wasted marketing efforts.

With the advent of AI, however, this landscape has drastically changed. Sophisticated machine learning algorithms now analyse vast amounts of data, from viewing histories to user interactions, to deliver highly personalised video content to individual users.

This not only enhances user engagement but also makes it easier for marketers to target their content more effectively, democratising the field and lowering the barriers to entry for newcomers.

Imagine this: you've just finished a long day at work or school, and you're looking to unwind with some quality video content. As you unlock your phone or boot up your smart TV, you're instantly bombarded by an avalanche of choices. Netflix tempts you with its latest big-budget drama series. Meanwhile, YouTube suggests a plethora of videos ranging from educational content to the latest viral sensations. TikTok's algorithm nags you to catch up on trending short-form videos, while Instagram Stories urge you to see what your friends are up to. In this digital maelstrom, making a choice feels like an insurmountable task. That's where Artificial Intelligence (AI) comes in.

AI is not just another buzzword; it's a transformative technology that has fundamentally altered the digital landscape, especially in the realm of video content. Gone are the days when viewers flipped through TV channels or scrolled aimlessly through a video-sharing site, hoping to stumble upon something engaging. Today, AI-enabled algorithms sift through vast libraries of content, analysing user behaviour, preferences, and even the time of day, to curate a bespoke list of video recommendations for each user.

This chapter aims to peel back the layers of complexity around how AI is shaping our video consumption habits. We'll delve into the science behind the algorithms that decide what you watch next, how these technologies keep viewers engaged, and what this means for the future of digital content and marketing. We're also going to explore some of the ethical considerations around AI and data usage, because, with great power comes great responsibility.

Most notably, this chapter will provide insights into how AI doesn't just make your video-watching experience more personalised but also more engaging and interactive. For instance, interactive storytelling experiences like Netflix's 'Bandersnatch' allow viewers to choose the direction of the story, and this too is informed by AI algorithms that have learned from millions of previous choices made by viewers. The line between creator and consumer is becoming increasingly blurred, thanks to AI.

Understanding the AI-driven mechanics of video content isn't just a curiosity; it's a necessity for anyone who creates, markets, or consumes digital content. As AI algorithms become more sophisticated, they're expected to play an even more significant role in shaping cultural narratives and consumer behaviours. Being aware of how these algorithms work and their broader implications can empower users to make more informed choices and help creators and marketers better engage with their target audiences.

6.1 The Mechanics of AI in Video Content Recommendation

Video recommendation systems are not mere tools; they are the engine that powers your user experience on any video platform. In essence, these algorithms are your digital concierge, guiding you through an almost infinite maze of content. These systems work in nuanced ways to dramatically boost user engagement and satisfaction by offering a personalised platter of videos.

For example, let's consider the behemoth video platform YouTube. When you log into YouTube, the first thing you see is a homepage filled with videos that the platform thinks you'd enjoy. Ever wondered how these recommendations are so spot on? That's the work of highly complex, multi-layered algorithms.

How Content Recommendation Systems Work

Different platforms may rely on one or multiple types of recommendation algorithms, each with its unique pros and cons. Let's break down some of the most prevalent methods:

Content-Based Filtering

This method employs domain-specific algorithms that create a 'profile' of each user based on their past interactions, preferences, and behavioural data. By analysing these features, the algorithm offers recommendations that closely align with what it 'thinks' the user will enjoy.

For instance, if you've recently watched several cooking shows on a platform, a content-based filtering system might suggest a newly-released documentary on the culinary arts. The aim is to encapsulate a user's interests in a mathematical vector and then find content that aligns with that vector.

Collaborative Filtering

Arguably the most widely used approach, collaborative filtering utilises a user-item interaction matrix. Imagine this matrix as a giant spreadsheet where each row is a user and each column is a video. The values in the cells are the ratings or interactions that users have had with videos. The system identifies patterns or 'clusters' of similar users and items to generate recommendations.

For example, if User A and User B have both liked and watched Videos X, Y, and Z, and User A also enjoyed Video W, it's highly likely that Video W will be recommended to User B.

Continuous Learning and Real-time Feedback

Contrary to static algorithms, AI-based recommendation systems have the capacity for continuous learning. Every like, dislike, comment, or even how long you watch a video contributes to real-time feedback loops that allow the algorithm to adapt.

Imagine watching a sports highlight reel but skipping every clip that involves basketball. Over time, the algorithm will 'learn' that you're less interested in basketball and more inclined to watch, say, football highlights.

Personalised Video Ranker

This is one of the more advanced types of recommendation algorithms, which customises your entire browsing experience, right down to the categories you see on your home screen. Imagine logging into a platform and finding an entire section dedicated to 'Films Based on Your Favourite Novels,'— that's the personalised video ranker at work.

Top N Video Ranker

Aiming for quality over quantity, this algorithm curates a list of the top videos for you based on predefined metrics, like engagement rates, click-through rates, or watch time. This is similar to how Spotify might offer you a 'Top Songs of the Year' playlist based on the tracks you've listened to the most.

Think of it as a 'highlight reel' of your content interactions, aiming to showcase only the crème de la crème of what the platform thinks you would enjoy.

Understanding the intricate mechanics of AI in video content recommendation is crucial for both consumers keen on maximising their viewing experience and marketers looking to tap into the vast potential of targeted content delivery. As AI technology continues to evolve, we can expect even more sophisticated layers of personalisation, engagement, and interactivity to come into play.

Deciphering social media algorithms is nothing short of cracking a complex code for digital marketers. This becomes particularly imperative when leveraging video as a medium. Social media platforms such as Facebook, Instagram, and Twitter are ever-changing landscapes, continually updating their algorithms to enhance user experience. For marketers, understanding these algorithms can mean the difference between a video going viral or falling flat.

Imagine launching a marketing campaign for a new product. Your videos may be high-quality and engaging, but if they don't align with the platforms' algorithms, they could easily get buried under a sea of content. Consequently, a nuanced understanding of these algorithms is crucial for maximum outreach and engagement.

Key Elements of Social Media Algorithms for Video

Different platforms employ various algorithms, but they often share some fundamental principles:

User Interactions

The more interaction—likes, shares, comments—a video receives, the more likely it is to be seen by a larger audience. Algorithms heavily weigh user engagement as a quality signal. In practical terms, let's say you're marketing an eco-friendly product. A video showcasing its unique selling points coupled with a call-to-action that prompts engagement ("like if you care about the planet") could gain substantial traction, thereby boosting its algorithmic ranking.

Content Relevance

If a user often engages with a particular type of content, algorithms note this preference and offer similar videos. If you're in the fashion industry, for example, your videos could be recommended to users who frequently engage with fashion content—even if they've never interacted with your brand before.

Timeliness

Newly uploaded videos generally receive preference. Posting a timely, topical video that aligns with current events or trending topics can give you a head-start in algorithmic ranking. For instance, posting a Christmas-themed video in December is likely to receive more algorithmic favour than in April.

Video Length and Completion Rates

Some platforms, like Instagram and Facebook, consider the video's length and how much of it is watched. If your video manages to retain viewers until the very end, it's an indicator of quality content, which in turn positively impacts its ranking. As an example, a 10-minute DIY tutorial with a high completion rate could outperform a shorter, less engaging clip.

Striking the Right Balance

Mastering the art of social media algorithms for video marketing is a balancing act. Your content should be captivating enough to hold the viewer's attention while simultaneously incorporating elements that resonate with algorithmic preferences. Therefore, marketers should keep track of evolving algorithmic trends and adapt their strategies accordingly.

For example, if short-form videos are gaining popularity on a platform like TikTok, a marketer might need to rethink their approach of primarily relying on longer formats. Likewise, if a platform introduces a new feature—say, Instagram introduces a new video format like 'Reels'—promptly utilising that format may offer an initial boost in algorithmic ranking.

Understanding and adapting to social media algorithms are essential steps for any digital marketer aiming to make the most of video content. It's not just about crafting compelling videos, but about strategically positioning them within the digital ecosystem for optimal visibility and engagement.

6.3 Dynamic Playlists through AI-Driven Search Engines

AI-driven search engines have become the linchpin for curating dynamic playlists that offer users an ever-evolving, personalised experience. Using a blend of machine learning algorithms and real-time data analytics, these search engines navigate through an extensive database of content, finding the gems that match a user's interests and behaviour. Think of it as having a personal DJ who not only knows your musical tastes but also keeps track of your mood and what's trending.

Elaborating on the Key Features of Dynamic Playlists

- **User Profiling**

This starts with a comprehensive understanding of a user's interaction history, from the genres they favour to how long they typically listen to a song or video. For instance, if you frequently listen to indie rock and occasionally dabble in classical music, the AI system captures this nuanced behaviour. Over time, as the system updates your profile, you might find that the playlist seamlessly blends indie tracks with modern classical pieces when you're working late at night.

- **Content Classification**

Using machine learning and deep learning technologies, dynamic playlists can perform content categorisation at a granular level. If a new indie rock song with classical undertones gets released, the system can identify and tag the song accordingly, making it a perfect candidate for your unique playlist.

- **Real-Time Adaptation**

The real beauty of dynamic playlists lies in their ability to adapt instantly. If it's Friday evening and you've been interacting with upbeat tracks, the AI can deduce that you're likely in the mood for more energetic music. Similarly, when a new album from your favourite artist drops, the system can automatically add it to your playlist, ensuring you're always up-to-date.

- **Cross-Platform Integration**

Imagine listening to a playlist on a music streaming service like Spotify, then switching over to a news site and finding a list of articles tailored to your interests. The key here is to provide a consistent and personalised experience across different platforms, making your digital life more seamless.

- **Discovery and Serendipity**

It's not all about sticking to the familiar; one of the most exciting features is the algorithm's ability to sprinkle in surprises. If you've been heavily into jazz lately, the system might throw in a classical piece performed by a jazz orchestra, broadening your horizons without jarring the flow of your playlist.

How to Create Your Dynamic Playlist with AI

1. **Choose the Platform**: The first step is to select a service that provides dynamic playlist features, be it Spotify, Apple Music, or a niche platform that caters to your unique taste.

2. **Input Preferences**: Initially, you may need to manually select genres, artists, or even specific songs to give the AI a starting point. The more data you provide, the more accurately the system can generate a playlist tailored just for you.

3. **Review Personalised Recommendations**: Almost instantaneously, a playlist will be generated. You can then listen, skip, like, or dislike songs, which further informs the algorithm.

4. **Refine Your Experience**: As you interact, the AI algorithm learns from your actions. If you skipped a particular track or liked another, these actions are logged to refine future recommendations, ensuring that your playlist remains dynamic and personalised.

Dynamic playlists driven by AI search engines are more than just a list of songs; they are a fluid, evolving soundscape curated to enrich your listening experience continually.

Chapter 7: Budget and ROI on AI Video Marketing

In traditional video marketing, budgeting and calculating the Return on Investment (ROI) have often been cumbersome tasks that required significant expertise.

From high production costs to the hiring of specialised staff for video editing, analytics, and market research, the financial barriers to entry were substantial. For small businesses and individual marketers, these costs often made effective video marketing strategies an unattainable goal.

However, AI technology is revolutionising this landscape. With AI-driven tools, the budgeting process is simplified, and calculating ROI becomes a more straightforward task. Even better, the production costs are substantially reduced due to automated processes like camera control, editing, and analytics.

This democratisation of video marketing means that even those with limited budgets can now achieve professional-level results, making the once-daunting challenge of budgeting and ROI management accessible to all.

The marriage between Artificial Intelligence (AI) and video marketing is nothing short of a digital renaissance. These two dynamic entities have converged to redefine user engagement and elevate content personalisation to unprecedented heights. However, beneath the sheen of technological marvels lies the gritty reality of economics. No matter how enticing AI capabilities may seem, the financial feasibility of integrating this technology is a concern for organisations. This chapter goes beyond the surface-level excitement around AI and video marketing to dig deep into its cost implications and how you can quantify your ROI

7.1 Cost-effectiveness of Using AI

The allure of cutting-edge technology like AI often comes with the presumption of exorbitant costs. Yet, this is an oversimplification. While initial costs can be high, the long-term efficiencies and potential for increased revenue can render AI a smart investment.

Initial Investment vs Long-term Savings

Embarking on an AI-powered video marketing venture necessitates initial investments in specialised software, skilled professionals, and data infrastructure. These preliminary costs can be daunting but should be viewed as a foundation for future savings and revenue generation.

Case Study: Automated Video Editing

Consider a company that previously relied on a team of five video editors, each working 40 hours per week, to generate promotional video content. With an AI-based automated editing tool, the workload could be reduced by 50%, freeing up employees to focus on more creative or strategic tasks.

Scalability

Traditional marketing solutions usually scale linearly, meaning that as your business grows, your expenses grow at a similar rate. AI, on the other hand, exhibits a non-linear scaling pattern. Essentially, as your user base or content volume increases, the incremental cost and resource allocation do not spike correspondingly.

Example: Streamlined Data Analysis

As your company scales, a traditional system may require you to hire more analysts to handle increased data. However, with an AI system that's already in place, it can manage larger data sets with little to no additional cost. The algorithm becomes more accurate as it has more data to learn from, enhancing its efficiency at no extra expense.

Real-time Adaptability

The dynamic nature of AI allows for real-time adjustments in your marketing strategies based on current user interactions and behaviors. This responsiveness ensures that your financial resources are being utilised to the fullest extent.

Real-world Application: Dynamic Ad Allocation

Suppose you have set aside a budget of £10,000 for video ads on social media platforms. A traditional approach would involve setting a fixed budget for each platform and waiting to evaluate performance. With AI, if one platform is generating more engagement, the system can automatically reallocate funds to accentuate this success, potentially reducing wasted ad spend by a significant margin.

By viewing the implementation of AI through the lens of long-term gains rather than just initial costs, businesses can gain a more accurate and encouraging perspective on the technology's financial viability. AI's scalability and real-time adaptability offer unique advantages, turning what may initially seem like an extravagant expense into a cost-effective investment.

7.2 ROI Metrics and KPIs

In the realm of AI video marketing, having a solid grasp of ROI metrics and Key Performance Indicators (KPIs) is non-negotiable for assessing the success of your campaigns. It's not about vague assumptions; it's about concrete data that paints a vivid picture of your investment's efficacy. Below, we go deeper into key metrics and KPIs, illustrating each with examples for better understanding.

Cost Per Acquisition (CPA)

CPA offers an immediate snapshot of your marketing efficiency by revealing the cost incurred to gain a new customer via your AI-powered video marketing initiatives.

Real-world Example:

If your CPA is £25 and you acquired 200 new customers last month, that means you spent £5,000 on your campaign. Understanding this figure in isolation might not be insightful, but comparing it to other campaigns or industry benchmarks can offer valuable perspectives.

Customer Lifetime Value (CLTV)

CLTV goes beyond the immediate transaction to examine the long-term value a customer brings over their entire life cycle. A campaign that effectively optimises CPA and CLTV will see a considerable ROI.

Case Study:

Imagine that the CLTV for your business is £300. If your CPA is £25, the margin between the two (£275) is the surplus value gained from each customer, indicative of a profitable AI investment.

Engagement Rates

Engagement metrics like likes, shares, and comments provide insights into how captivating your AI-generated video content is. Higher engagement typically correlates with higher conversion rates, thus positively influencing ROI.

Practical Scenario:

If your recent AI-driven video received 10,000 views with 1,000 likes and 500 shares, these are strong indicators of audience interest and potential for conversion.

Conversion Rate

The ultimate measure of your campaign's potency is the conversion rate. This metric reveals the percentage of viewers who performed a desired action, such as making a purchase or signing up for a newsletter, after watching your video.

For Instance:

If out of 10,000 viewers, 500 ended up making a purchase, your conversion rate would be 5%. High conversion rates usually signify that your AI algorithms are effectively targeting and messaging your audience.

ROI Calculation

Calculating ROI synthesises all the above metrics into one comprehensible figure. The formula is straightforward:

ROI= (Net profit / Cost of investment) x 100

Sample Calculation:

Suppose your net profit from an AI-driven campaign was £20,000, and your investment cost was £5,000. Your ROI would be (20000 / 5000)×100 = 400, a 4x profit - a clear indicator of a highly successful campaign!

By meticulously tracking these ROI metrics and KPIs, you can assess the impact and profitability of your AI video marketing strategies. This data-driven approach allows you to validate your investment in AI technology and aids in future decision-making, ensuring that your marketing budget is aligned with your business objectives effectively.

Chapter 8: Enhancing Visual Appeal with AI - An Expanded Insight

In traditional marketing, enhancing the visual appeal of video content has often been a complex and costly affair, requiring specialized skills in graphic design, video editing, and animation.

For small businesses or individual entrepreneurs, these requirements could represent significant barriers to entry. However, the advent of AI technology has been a game-changer in this domain. AI-driven tools now offer automated solutions for video enhancement, such as intelligent colour grading, automated framing, and even real-time special effects.

These tools are often intuitive and user-friendly, drastically reducing the learning curve and financial investment needed to produce visually stunning video content. In essence, AI is democratising the world of video marketing, making it accessible for everyone, irrespective of their technical proficiency or budget constraints.

In an age where our digital existence is flooded with content and information, capturing the user's attention has never been more challenging, nor more crucial. Websites are the digital storefronts for businesses, making them the initial touchpoint for customer engagement. Aesthetically pleasing design and visual elements are no longer a luxury but a necessity. As attention spans shrink and the user becomes more discerning, the importance of an eye-catching website design has grown exponentially. Businesses have a mere matter of seconds to engage a visitor, and failure to do so can lead to lost opportunities.

Enter Artificial Intelligence (AI)—a revolutionary technology that is not only elevating the functional capabilities of websites but also their visual aesthetics. AI contributes to creating a cohesive and visually striking experience, transforming how the user interacts with the digital world. Its benefits extend from increased user engagement and improved accessibility to an enriched overall user experience. Let's delve deeper into how AI plays a transformative role in reshaping the norms of visual design.

AI's Transformative Role in Visual Design: A Paradigm Shift

The integration of AI into visual design is essentially rewriting the rulebook on aesthetics and engagement. In a traditional setting, the creation of visually appealing websites was often a subjective process, governed by the designer's intuition and client preferences. While expertise in visual theory and design principles will always be important, AI offers data-driven insights that make this subjective process more objective and consumer-centric.

For example, AI algorithms can analyze thousands of websites and come up with design features that are statistically more likely to engage a user. Therefore, instead of a "hit and miss" approach, designers equipped with AI tools can produce a design that has quantifiable impact factors. Imagine a clothing retailer incorporating an AI tool that can adjust the visual elements on its homepage based on real-time data of user interactions, thereby providing a dynamic and personalised shopping experience.

One of the key aspects of an engaging digital environment is the user interface (UI), the gateway through which interactions between humans and machines occur. The significance of intuitive UIs cannot be overstated; they form the foundation of the user's journey on a website.

AI significantly contributes to this by analysing a multitude of factors like eye movement, scrolling patterns, and mouse clicks to offer data-driven suggestions for optimal design layouts. A classic example here would be a news aggregator site that uses AI to understand what type of news categories attract the most reader attention. Based on this data, the UI can dynamically prioritize the display of these categories, thereby increasing user engagement.

Customization and personalisation have emerged as significant trends in recent years, affecting everything from content to design elements. The one-size-fits-all approach is fading into obsolescence. AI technologies like machine learning and data analytics can process vast amounts of user data to create a highly personalised experience.

For instance, a fitness platform could use AI to determine what type of workout regimes or diet plans are most frequently clicked or viewed by a user. Consequently, the next time that user visits the site, the homepage could highlight similar or related fitness plans, making the user feel understood and catered to.

Beyond just colours, fonts, and layouts, AI can take visual design to the next level by setting new benchmarks in user engagement. It does this by understanding the deeper nuances of how visual elements impact user psychology. Machine learning models can analyse which visual elements cause users to stay longer on a webpage, thus aiding in reducing bounce rates.

Consider an e-commerce website that utilises AI to adapt in real-time to user behaviour. If the AI algorithm determines that a user is likely to leave the website, it can immediately trigger a pop-up featuring a visually compelling special offer. The goal here is not merely to entice but to engage the user in a way that feels organic and fluid.

AI's role in the domain of visual design isn't a mere additive; it's a transformative force that is revolutionising the way businesses think about and implement design strategies. AI tools provide an insightful, data-driven, and personalised approach to web design, elevating not just the visual aesthetics but also enriching the holistic user experience. The confluence of AI and design is an exciting frontier that is set to redefine the digital landscapes of tomorrow.

8.1 Incorporating AI for Video Visual Effects - A Deeper Dive

The ubiquity of video content in today's digital landscape cannot be overstated. Videos are no longer just another form of entertainment; they have become an indispensable tool for storytelling, marketing, and driving user engagement. Artificial Intelligence (AI) is increasingly stepping into this space, bringing transformative changes in the way we create, edit, and interact with video content. In this section, we'll delve deeper into the wide array of applications of AI in video visual effects.

Automated Editing: The Future of Post-Production

Automated video editing, enabled by AI, has evolved as a game-changer in the realm of post-production. Gone are the days when editors had to manually trawl through hours of footage, fine-tuning colours and sound levels.

Consider AI tools like Lumen5, which can convert a blog post or a news article into a captivating video, complete with appropriate visuals and background music. The AI algorithm takes care of colour correction, sound balancing, and even text overlay. This automated sophistication frees the creators from mundane and repetitive tasks, empowering them to invest more time in creative ideation and storytelling.

Personalised Content Creation: The Ultimate User Magnet

Personalisation is no longer just a buzzword; it's the secret sauce that significantly boosts user engagement and content retention. AI technologies can sift through enormous volumes of user data to generate videos that are not just eye-catching but deeply personalised.

Imagine an e-commerce platform that uses AI to analyse the browsing and purchasing history of its users. The system could auto-generate short, personalised video recommendations for related products and send these clips directly to the user's inbox or feature them on the homepage, thereby substantially increasing the odds of sales conversion.

Scriptwriting: The AI Muse

AI in scriptwriting is revolutionising the way narratives are crafted. These tools are no longer mere text generators; they are intelligent systems that can aid in plot development, character arc creation, and even conflict resolution.

AI tools like ShortlyAI can emulate the style of renowned authors, offering struggling scriptwriters a burst of inspiration. Such tools can even help in avoiding plot holes or generating compelling dialogues, making the writing process more dynamic and less cumbersome.

Voice Acting: Cutting Costs, Not Quality

The development of text-to-speech technology is giving voice to videos like never before. High-quality voiceovers are now achievable without the associated costs of hiring professional voice actors or booking recording studios.

Google's Text-to-Speech API has drastically improved the quality of computer-generated audio, adding nuances such as pitch variation and timing, which make the voiceovers sound astonishingly natural. This enables video content to be effortlessly localised into multiple languages, widening its global reach.

Real-time Analytics: The Instant Report Card

The power of AI-driven analytics extends to immediate, real-time feedback on video content performance. These insights are not just about views and likes; they provide a comprehensive understanding of audience engagement.

For example, YouTube Studio offers an AI-generated analytics dashboard that displays key metrics, including watch time and like-to-dislike ratios. It can even indicate the exact moments in a video where viewers are most likely to disengage, thus providing crucial data for content optimisation.

Content Moderation: The Guardian Angel

The digital space is not devoid of risks, making content moderation crucial. AI tools can automatically detect and remove inappropriate or harmful content, ensuring a safer user experience.

Platforms like Netra utilise AI to scan videos for malicious or inappropriate content. Be it hate speech, violence, or explicit material, these tools can flag them for review or remove them altogether, making the digital ecosystem a safer space for interaction.

Efficiency and Time Optimisation: Work Smarter, Not Harder

AI offers unprecedented advantages in speeding up the video editing process. From automated tagging to intelligent transcribing, AI technologies have covered all bases.

Descript is an example of an AI tool that quickly transcribes video content, allowing creators to edit the video simply by editing the transcript text. This is especially beneficial for summarising longer pieces of content or for generating subtitles, thereby making the content more accessible.

The role of AI in video visual effects is not just complementary; it's transformative. From creating intelligent automated edits to enabling hyper-personalised content and real-time analytics, AI is setting new industry standards. Its impact extends beyond mere technical enhancements, bringing a paradigm shift in quality, efficiency, and creativity. With these advancements, we are standing at the cusp of a new era in digital storytelling.

8.2 AI Techniques for Image and Scene Recognition: Transforming Visual Perception

The impact of Artificial Intelligence (AI) in the domain of image and scene recognition is both far-reaching and revolutionary. It has shattered traditional limitations, offering a myriad of applications from advanced facial recognition systems to automated enhancements for visual content. Here, we will deep-dive into the technology behind this revolution.

The Fundamentals of Image Processing

To fully comprehend the transformative role of AI, one must first understand the basics of image processing. Broadly, image processing can be categorised into two types: Analog and Digital.

Analog Image Processing:
Analog image processing involves the manipulation of continuous signals. This can mean tweaking brightness and contrast levels directly on a physical photograph or through analog electronic equipment.

Digital Image Processing:
Digital image processing, on the other hand, operates on the pixel-based representation of

an image. Algorithms are used to manipulate or enhance images, from simple tasks like cropping to complex operations like object recognition.

Leading Techniques in AI Image Recognition

Various AI techniques have redefined what's possible in image processing. Among these, Convolutional Neural Networks (CNNs), Deep Learning, Generative Adversarial Networks (GANs), and Transformer Networks are the most impactful.

Convolutional Neural Networks (CNNs): The Pattern Masters

CNNs consist of layers of artificial neurons designed to recognise patterns in images. By using a series of filters and transformations, these networks can identify shapes, textures, and other features.

For example:
Facial recognition software used in modern smartphones employs CNNs to identify specific patterns in your face, distinguishing it from millions of others with incredible accuracy. Additionally, in healthcare, CNNs are being used to identify anomalies in X-rays and MRI scans.

Deep Learning: The Autonomous Learner

Deep Learning technologies utilise deep neural networks to automatically learn to represent data. They are especially adept at understanding complex structures and hierarchies in an image.

Case in Point:
Deep Learning is used in wildlife conservation efforts where it assists in identifying endangered species in numerous photos captured by camera traps, thereby aiding in population tracking and study.

Generative Adversarial Networks (GANs): The Realism Generators

GANs function with two competing neural networks, one for generating data and the other for evaluating it. This generates incredibly realistic images, often indistinguishable from actual photos.

Example:
Artists and graphic designers use GANs to create photorealistic scenes, sometimes even synthesising pictures of people who do not exist but look convincingly real.

Transformer Networks: The Multi-Domain Experts

Also known as Vision Transformers (ViTs), these networks are versatile, capable of synthesising and manipulating data across different domains, including both text and images.

Scenario:
A fashion e-commerce site could use Vision Transformers to automatically match product

descriptions with corresponding images, ensuring that the right products are displayed alongside accurate descriptions, thus enhancing user experience.

The Paradigm Shift in Visual Processing

AI's advent in image and scene recognition signifies more than just technological advancement; it represents a seismic shift in capabilities. The technology is not merely optimising existing processes; it is creating entirely new possibilities. From facial recognition to artistic creation, from medical diagnostics to automated retail experiences, AI's applications are virtually limitless. With such a broad spectrum of applications, AI is not only enriching visual aesthetics but is also contributing to enhancing functionality and user engagement. By leveraging these transformative technologies, creators and businesses can redefine innovation in the visual domain, pushing boundaries like never before.

Chapter 9: Revolutionising Audio Production and Storytelling with AI

In the realm of audio production and storytelling, the traditional barriers to entry have been high, often requiring specialised equipment, software, and technical expertise. This made it challenging for small businesses or individual creators to produce high-quality audio content without substantial investment.

With the advent of AI technologies, however, these barriers are crumbling. AI-powered tools now enable automated mixing, mastering, and even content creation, obviating the need for specialized skills in sound engineering. Moreover, AI can assist in scriptwriting and storytelling, transforming a simple idea into a compelling narrative.

These technological advancements democratise the audio production landscape, making it more accessible and cost-effective for everyone.

The integration of Artificial Intelligence (AI) into the arena of audio production and vocal storytelling heralds a pivotal transformation in how we approach and utilise technology. Far from being a mere gimmick, AI's capabilities in crafting realistic voiceovers and speech synthesis have become indispensable in modern media and technology, changing the traditional paradigms of interaction and creativity.

9.1 AI-Powered Speech Synthesis and Voice Cloning: A New Frontier in Vocal Expression

Over the last few years, advancements in AI-powered speech synthesis and voice cloning have evolved from intriguing experiments to groundbreaking, real-world applications. Far from just being a spectacle of technological might, these capabilities are potent tools that offer nuanced ways of personalising and interacting with vocal mediums. In this context, the technology is reshaping entertainment, marketing, accessibility, and even our emotional connection to voices.

Why Is AI Voice Cloning Being Utilised?

AI voice cloning technology is incredibly versatile, with a vast range of applications that meet various needs across different sectors:

Budget-Friendly Solutions: In a world where budgets are often constrained, employing human voice actors for every project can prove to be a costly affair. AI voice cloning offers a budget-friendly alternative. For example, small businesses can use AI-generated voiceovers for their promotional videos, thereby saving costs on hiring professional talent.

Round-the-Clock Availability: Unlike human voice actors who have schedules and availability constraints, AI offers a 24/7 'voice actor' at your disposal. This perpetual availability proves invaluable for time-sensitive projects, such as news bulletins or urgent public announcements.

Personal Archives and Emotional Continuity: Perhaps one of the most poignant applications is the capability to recreate voices of individuals who are no longer with us. By providing the AI with a sample of the voice, families can, in a way, preserve the auditory essence of a loved one for posterity.

Applications of Voice Cloning

Personalisation: One of the first sectors to adopt AI voice cloning was the world of virtual assistants. Imagine a virtual assistant that speaks in the voice of your favourite actor, or even a deceased family member. This offers a more personal, emotionally-engaging interaction with the technology.

Entertainment: In the realm of film and gaming, voice cloning provides unparalleled creative freedoms. For instance, filmmakers can resurrect the voices of historical figures for documentaries, adding authenticity and gravitas. Meanwhile, game developers can offer an array of dynamic, emotionally responsive characters, improving the gaming experience immeasurably.

Accessibility: For individuals who have lost their ability to speak due to medical conditions, AI-powered voice synthesis can give them a voice quite literally. For example, individuals suffering from conditions like ALS can still communicate using synthesised versions of their original voice, making the technology not just practical but also emotionally significant.

Content Creation: Marketing professionals and content creators are also capitalising on voice cloning. From generating brand-aligned voiceovers for advertisements to narrating e-books in the author's own 'voice,' the applications are wide-ranging and impactful.

Advantages of Voice Cloning

Cost-Efficiency: Voice cloning technology eliminates the need for repetitive, expensive studio sessions. This is crucial for businesses operating on tight budgets.

Customisation: Voice cloning allows for an extraordinary level of customisation. For example, marketing professionals can tweak the pitch, tempo, or emotion of the AI-generated voice to align perfectly with brand ethos.

Accessibility: For those with speech disabilities, providing a sample of their voice allows for the synthesis of a communication tool tailored precisely for them, enhancing both their quality of life and social interactions.

AI Voice Cloning Tools

Murf: Known for its realistic emotional range, Murf offers custom voice clones that express emotions from anger and happiness to sadness. It's a favourite among podcasters and digital marketers aiming to add a layer of emotional depth to their content.

LOVO: Adopted by thousands of businesses and content creators, LOVO not only provides highly realistic voices but also offers a selection of 25+ emotional nuances. This versatility makes it ideal for crafting compelling narratives in audio-visual presentations.

ReadSpeaker: Focusing primarily on text-to-speech capabilities, ReadSpeaker is a reliable tool for those in need of accurate voice cloning. Its proficiency lies in its ability to closely match the sample voice, making it a trustworthy option for a range of applications, from audiobooks to customer service bots.

AI-powered speech synthesis and voice cloning are more than just technological novelties. They are revolutionising the way we engage with audio media, offering unprecedented levels of personalisation, efficiency, and emotional resonance. As these technologies continue to mature, they promise to reshape our interaction with the auditory world in ways we are only beginning to understand.

9.2 AI-Generated Voiceovers in Videos

The advent of AI-generated voiceovers is undeniably a game-changer in the landscape of video production. Thanks to the advanced algorithms employed in deep learning and neural networks, AI can simulate human-like voices with astonishing accuracy. By examining vast datasets comprising human speech, these AI models grasp the subtleties of tone, pitch, and emphasis, thereby allowing you to convert text into remarkably realistic audio. As the technology ingests more data, it continues to refine its ability to mimic the intricacies of human speech.

How Are AI Voices Created?

Deep learning technologies and neural networks are at the heart of AI-generated voices. These algorithms trawl through extensive speech databases to decode the intricate nuances of human conversation, right down to the minor details like inflection and tone. For example, when you input text to be converted to speech, the AI employs its learned knowledge to produce an audio output that closely resembles a human voice. Think of it as an incredibly advanced form of text-to-speech, informed by a comprehensive understanding of how humans actually talk. The more speech data the AI analyses, the better its generated voices become at sounding like an authentic human.

Cloning Human Voices: A Double-Edged Sword

While the capabilities of AI-generated voiceovers are awe-inspiring, they come with potential downsides, particularly for the industry of human voice actors.

- **Threat to Livelihood**: Voice actors have traditionally relied on the uniqueness of their voices to secure work. The advent of AI systems that can replicate human voices poses a significant threat to this profession. There are even instances where AI has been used to clone voice actors' unique styles, effectively 'stealing' their voice.

- **Market Competition**: Due to their low cost, AI-generated voiceovers can undercut human voice actors dramatically. For example, an AI system could offer hundreds of hours of narration at a fraction of what it would cost to hire a human, making it increasingly difficult for traditional voice actors to compete.

Benefits of AI-Generated Voiceovers in Videos

Cost-Effective

Engaging professional voice talent can be a hefty line item in a project budget. AI-generated voiceovers, by contrast, are a cost-effective solution. For startups or creators on a budget, this can free up funds for other aspects of production.

Efficiency

In traditional settings, coordinating with human voice actors can be time-consuming, particularly if retakes or edits are needed. AI-generated voiceovers can be produced in mere minutes, allowing for faster turnaround times and thereby accelerating the overall video production process.

Customisation

The technology allows you to tweak the voice to align with your brand identity or the thematic elements of your video. You can select from a wide array of accents, tones, and even emotional nuances.

Multilingual Support

AI-generated voices can speak multiple languages fluently, opening up your content to global audiences. For instance, you could produce a marketing video in English and easily repurpose it for a French or Spanish-speaking audience without the need to hire additional voice talent.

Types of Voiceovers for Videos

1. **Voice Actor Voiceovers**: Despite the benefits of AI, human voice actors still hold the upper hand in delivering highly emotive or nuanced performances. For storytelling that requires a deep emotional connection, the human touch remains irreplaceable.

2. **Self-Recorded Voiceovers**: With the right equipment and software, self-recording is another viable option. This approach is particularly useful for vloggers or content creators who prefer a more personal touch in their videos.

3. **AI Voiceovers (Text-to-Speech)**: AI-generated voices are becoming ubiquitous. They range from virtual assistants like Siri and Alexa to GPS navigation systems. With text-to-speech technology, using AI-generated voices for video voiceovers is now standard practice.

Potential Use Cases

- **Explainer Videos**: Break down complex topics into easily digestible content. For example, a tech startup could utilise an AI voiceover to guide viewers through how their new software works.

- **E-Learning**: Supplement educational videos with AI-generated narration to keep learners engaged. These could be used in everything from corporate training modules to university courses.

- **Marketing Videos**: Amplify your brand's message in commercials or product showcases. You can align the AI voice to suit your brand's tone and style, whether it be formal, casual, or anywhere in between.

- **Documentaries**: Enhance the viewer experience by adding context and commentary via AI narration. For example, a historical documentary could use AI to emulate the voice of a significant figure from the period being discussed.

- **Content Localization**: AI voiceovers enable you to effortlessly adapt your video content to cater to diverse linguistic and cultural demographics, without having to record multiple versions.

AI-generated voiceovers offer a blend of cost-efficiency, speed, and customisation that is radically transforming video production across multiple sectors. While they may not entirely replace the emotional depth a human actor can offer, their growing versatility and quality make them an invaluable tool in the modern content creator's arsenal.

9.3 Ethical Implications of Voice Cloning

The revolutionary advancement of voice cloning technology brings to the fore several ethical concerns that need careful consideration. As voice cloning is increasingly integrated into various aspects of modern life, from personal AI assistants to voiceovers in documentaries, the ethical landscape grows more complicated.

Identity and Consent

- **Unauthorized Voice Cloning**: One of the most pressing ethical issues is the potential for unauthorised cloning of an individual's voice. In a world where one's vocal identity can be replicated with just a few samples, the consequences could be dire. For instance, your voice could be used without your permission in a political campaign, or even for committing fraud.

- **Consent from the Deceased**: The technology enables us to resurrect the voices of individuals who have passed away. While this may offer comfort to loved ones, it raises questions about the ethicality of using someone's voice without their explicit consent, something that's impossible to obtain posthumously.

Economic Implications

- **Job Security for Voice Actors**: As previously discussed, AI-generated voices pose a significant threat to human voice actors. As AI technologies become more sophisticated, the unique attributes that make human voice actors irreplaceable could be mimicked, jeopardising their livelihood.

- **Fair Pricing**: If AI can produce the same quality of voiceovers at a fraction of the cost, what is the ethical stance on pricing? The undercutting of human labor raises questions about fair pricing and ethical business practices.

Privacy and Data Security

- **Data Misuse**: Voice data used for cloning could be misused if it falls into the wrong hands. Scenarios range from the relatively innocuous, such as unwanted advertising, to the more sinister, like blackmail or identity theft.

- **Ownership**: Who owns the rights to a cloned voice? If a voice actor's vocal characteristics are cloned, do they have a claim to the intellectual property that is subsequently produced using that cloned voice?

Social and Cultural Concerns

- **Misinformation**: The potential for spreading misinformation using cloned voices is significant. Imagine a situation where a public figure's voice is cloned to disseminate false statements—this could have far-reaching consequences on public opinion and even national security.

- **Cultural Appropriation**: As AI allows for the cloning and altering of accents and dialects, there is a risk of cultural appropriation or misrepresentation. For example, using a British accent to lend an air of authority to a cloned voice in an American setting may propagate stereotypes.

Regulatory Framework

- **Legal Oversight**: As it stands, the legal landscape surrounding voice cloning is murky at best. Governments and regulatory bodies have yet to catch up with the rapid advancements in AI voice technology. Clear regulations and laws need to be established to govern the ethical use of voice cloning.

Ethical Guidelines and Industry Standards

- **Transparency**: One possible ethical guideline is to make it obligatory for AI-generated voices to disclose their synthetic nature when interacting with humans. This allows the audience to differentiate between human and AI voices and make informed decisions accordingly.

- **Quality Control**: Setting industry standards for the ethical use of voice cloning technology could serve as a safeguard against potential misuse. These standards could outline the parameters for consent, data security, and fair business practices.

The ethical implications of voice cloning are far-reaching and multifaceted. While the technology offers promising advancements in fields ranging from entertainment to assistive technologies, a balanced approach that addresses ethical concerns is imperative for its responsible integration into society.

Chapter 10: AI-Generated Video Thumbnails: The Nexus of Algorithms, Aesthetics, and Audience Engagement

In traditional video marketing, creating compelling thumbnails has often been a challenging task requiring a keen eye for design and an understanding of human psychology.

The thumbnail is not just an image; it's a visual handshake inviting the viewer to engage with the content. Designing an effective thumbnail usually involves graphic design skills, A/B testing, and ongoing adjustments to align with audience preferences, all of which can be time-consuming and costly.

This presents a barrier to entry for small businesses or individual content creators who may lack the resources for such intricate work. Enter AI-generated video thumbnails: By leveraging machine learning algorithms that analyse video content and audience behaviour, AI tools can automatically generate thumbnails that are not only visually appealing but also tailored to attract your specific target audience.

This technological advance simplifies the thumbnail creation process, making effective video marketing more accessible to everyone.

In an era awash with digital stimuli, from buzzing social media feeds to an ever-growing glut of online articles, the role of artificial intelligence (AI) in shaping our digital interactions is inescapable.

From search engine rankings to the intimate curation of personalised playlists on music streaming platforms, AI not only influences what we see but also steers how we engage with content. Amid this surfeit of digital choices, one area where AI is making an indelible impact is in the creation of video thumbnails.

These thumbnails act as the sentinels of your content, playing the dual role of gatekeepers and promoters. They are the determinants in the split-second decision-making process of whether to click and engage with a video or let it scroll into digital oblivion.

10.1 The Indelible Impact of AI-Generated Thumbnails on Click-Through Rates

Navigating the online world today is akin to strolling through an expansive, bustling bazaar, teeming with a myriad of wares vying for your attention. In this digital marketplace, video thumbnails serve as your storefront window display; they are the visual appetisers that tempt the audience to partake in the full course—the video itself.

The significance of these diminutive images is amplified by our neurological predisposition towards visual stimuli. The human brain can interpret a visual scene in just 13 milliseconds, underlining the need for an impactful thumbnail that can capture fleeting attention spans within this minuscule timeframe.

Advantages of AI in Thumbnail Creation

- **Minimisation of Human Error**

In the realm of human creativity, intuition and subjectivity often reign supreme. However, these very attributes can lead to oversights and inconsistencies. Unlike human judgement, which may be influenced by a variety of factors including mood or fatigue, AI algorithms dissect video content with a surgical precision that is devoid of human error. For instance, an AI model could scan hours of footage to identify moments of peak emotional intensity, be it a celebratory goal in a football match or the climax in a dramatic scene, thereby ensuring that the chosen frame is objectively engaging.

- **Risk Mitigation**

Beyond mere selection, AI technologies enable real-time experimentation, a feature that would be overwhelmingly laborious for human operators. The AI can continuously update thumbnails based on actual viewer engagement metrics, assessing in real-time what works and what doesn't. If a thumbnail featuring a cat achieves higher clicks over one featuring a dog, the algorithm will adjust future thumbnails accordingly. This agility in optimisation keeps the content not only fresh but perpetually fine-tuned to viewer preferences.

- **Digital Assistance**

In the age of digital customer service, AI-powered chatbots have evolved into incredibly sophisticated interfaces. These digital aides can handle an array of queries and even recommend related content. Imagine a user pausing over a thumbnail; the chatbot could instantly pop up and offer a snippet or review of the video, thereby increasing the likelihood of a click-through. This level of user engagement saves human customer service agents for more intricate or nuanced issues that require the human touch.

Influence on Click-Through Rates (CTR)

- **Personalised Marketing**

Gone are the days when one-size-fits-all thumbnails could achieve universal appeal. Today's AI technologies can craft thumbnails tailored to individual user profiles. By analysing user metrics such as browsing history, engagement rates, and demographic data, AI can create custom thumbnails that resonate with specific audiences. For example, a video on climate change could feature a thumbnail with a melting glacier for an environmentally-conscious audience, while depicting industrial emissions for a corporate audience, thereby maximising the video's reach and impact.

- **24/7 Customer Support via Chatbots**

The ubiquity of chatbots means that users can have their queries addressed immediately, at any hour of the day. This non-stop customer support not only improves user experience but also builds trust. The indirect benefit is an increase in CTR as users feel more comfortable and engaged within the platform.

- **Fraud Detection**

In a digital landscape rife with scams and fraudulent activities, maintaining a safe user environment is crucial. AI algorithms have become remarkably adept at flagging and neutralising threats, such as phishing attempts disguised as legitimate video content. By offering a secure platform, businesses not only protect their users but also bolster trust, which can result in an uptick in CTR.

By intertwining algorithms with aesthetics, and meshing them seamlessly into the fabric of audience preferences and behaviours, AI-generated video thumbnails represent the nexus where technology meets human engagement. The result is a transformative and highly personalised user experience, redefining how we interact with, and consume, digital video content in this AI-driven age.

10.2 The Realm of Possibilities: Thumbnails of the Future

As we stand at the frontier of AI innovation, the realm of video thumbnails beckons with a treasure trove of unexplored possibilities. This expanding digital frontier offers several avenues to redefine what we consider to be the status quo in user engagement.

Hyper-Personalisation

The current landscape of digital media consumption is on the cusp of a personalisation revolution. Imagine a YouTube interface where the thumbnail of a travel vlog shows the beaches of Bali to someone who's been searching for tropical vacations, while it shifts to a bustling Tokyo street scene for a viewer who's a fan of Japanese culture. The thumbnail morphs in real-time, adapting to the viewer's personal preferences and previous searches. This hyper-personalisation would not only capture interest more effectively but also ramp up click-through rates significantly.

Interactive Thumbnails

The static nature of thumbnails could soon become a relic of the past. As technology advances, we may see the emergence of interactive thumbnails that function as mini-demos. For example, hovering over a thumbnail might trigger a brief sequence of highlights from the video or present an interactive slideshow. Clicking could reveal statistics or key quotes related to the video content. This added layer of interactivity provides viewers with a richer, more informative preview, encouraging a deeper level of engagement even before the video is played.

Ethical Thumbnail Design

As the capabilities of AI expand, ethical considerations will inevitably come into sharper focus. For instance, how do we prevent thumbnails from misleading viewers or exploiting psychological triggers such as FOMO (Fear of Missing Out)? As AI matures, it's conceivable that ethical guidelines will be incorporated into the algorithms themselves, ensuring that thumbnails neither deceive nor manipulate but provide an accurate and fair representation of the video content.

While AI opens up a plethora of opportunities, it also poses its own set of challenges and ethical quandaries.

Ethical Quandaries

In the bid to attract viewer attention, there exists a fine line between enticement and manipulation. Thumbnails that are too sensationalised could be deemed as "clickbait," leading to ethical concerns around consent and transparency. This issue necessitates the development of ethical frameworks to guide AI algorithms in creating thumbnails that are both engaging and honest.

Overreliance on Automation

There's a risk that the human touch could be phased out if we lean too heavily on automation. While machine-generated thumbnails might be more data-driven, they lack the nuance and creativity that come from human intuition. Therefore, finding a harmonious interplay between human creativity and machine precision will be a critical factor in preserving the authenticity of digital content.

Data Privacy

As algorithms delve deeper into personalisation, the risk surrounding the handling of sensitive user data amplifies. Transparent data policies and robust security protocols will need to be in place to ensure that personal information is not misused or compromised.

10.4 Cutting-Edge Designing with AI

The abilities of contemporary AI models, including generative and foundational AI, extend far beyond mere thumbnail creation.

Content Personalisation

AI technology is increasingly enabling content creators to tailor not just thumbnails but entire videos to specific audience niches. For example, a video covering a general topic like "Healthy Eating" could automatically adjust its content—such as recipes or nutritional tips— based on the dietary preferences or restrictions of the viewer.

Automated Content Generation

Beyond thumbnails and videos, AI also holds promise in automating other forms of content generation. For businesses that need to churn out regular blog posts, articles, or social media updates, AI can handle the bulk of these tasks. This automation frees up human resources to focus on strategy, creativity, and tasks that require complex decision-making.

Quality and Diversity of Content

AI's ability to sift through enormous data sets allows it to discern trends and insights that might escape even the most seasoned human analysts. For example, if a certain video style or topic is becoming increasingly popular in a specific demographic, AI algorithms could detect this trend early on. Content creators can then produce videos that not only meet but anticipate audience demand, thereby driving both the quality and diversity of the content to new heights.

As we venture further into this AI-driven digital landscape, the way we conceptualise, produce, and engage with content will undergo transformative shifts. These emerging technologies and ethical considerations represent not just challenges but opportunities to create a more dynamic, interactive, and responsible digital media ecosystem.

10.5 AI in Thumbnail Design: A Paradigm Shift

The incursion of AI into the realm of thumbnail design isn't just an evolutionary step; it's a complete paradigm shift that revolutionises how thumbnails are crafted, displayed, and interacted with. Let's delve into each transformative element:

Image Selection and Enhancement

The traditional process of selecting a thumbnail often involves sifting through numerous frames to find one that seems appealing or relevant. AI goes a step further by scanning the entire video and picking the most relevant frames based on pre-determined criteria like emotional impact, subject focus, or visual clarity. But the AI doesn't stop there; it can also apply real-time enhancements like color correction, sharpening, or even adding dynamic elements to the thumbnail. For example, if the video is about cooking, AI could pick a frame showing the final dish and then enhance the image to make the colours pop, making it far more appealing at a glance.

Captivating Headlines

Headlines or titles have always played an essential role in capturing attention. AI algorithms have the capacity to evaluate the core themes of the video content and craft headlines that are both eye-catching and contextually relevant. For a news video on climate change, the algorithm might generate a headline like "Unveiling the Stark Reality of Melting Glaciers" instead of a more generic "Climate Change News," thereby attracting viewers who are specifically interested in the environmental impacts of global warming.

Video Previews

While static images have been the industry standard, we are on the cusp of welcoming AI-generated video previews as an option for thumbnails. These would be micro-trailers, maybe 2-3 seconds long, that give a whirlwind tour of the video's core content. For instance, a video on a 30-day fitness challenge might have a thumbnail that cycles through quick clips of Day 1, Day 15, and Day 30 transformations, enticing viewers to click and watch the journey.

Audience Personalisation

AI's true prowess lies in its ability to understand and adapt to individual user behaviour. By analysing browsing history, clicks, and even dwell time on certain videos, AI can dynamically adjust the thumbnail you see. So, if you're a history buff who frequently watches documentaries, the thumbnail for a video titled "The World Wars" might show an iconic image of Winston Churchill for you, whereas it could display battlefield scenes for someone more interested in military tactics.

AI-generated video thumbnails are not merely incremental upgrades; they signal a profound shift in the way digital content is discovered, engaged with, and enjoyed. These intelligent systems usher in a new era where thumbnails become adaptive, contextual, and remarkably efficient at capturing human attention.

As AI algorithms grow increasingly sophisticated, they will push the boundaries of what's possible, transforming static thumbnails into dynamic visual summaries, imbued with contextual understanding and personal relevance.

Far from being simple gatekeepers, these next-generation thumbnails will serve as interactive portals, guiding us into digital experiences that are richer, more personalised, and infinitely more captivating.

Checklist for using AI to generate and analyse your thumbnails:

Preliminary Planning:

1. **Define Objectives**: Understand what you want to achieve with your AI-generated thumbnails, such as increased click-through rates (CTR) or better user engagement.

2. **Identify Target Audience**: Know who your content is geared towards to make the thumbnails as effective as possible.

Platform Selection:

3. **Research Existing Platforms**: Look into platforms like TubeBuddy, vidIQ, or Google's AutoML Vision for thumbnail generation capabilities.

4. **Platform Comparison**: Weigh the pros and cons, pricing, and capabilities of each to find the best fit.

5. **Trial Period**: Utilise any free trials to understand the capabilities and limitations of the platform.

Data Gathering:

6. **Baseline Metrics**: Gather data on your current thumbnails' performance to serve as a comparison point.

7. **User Data**: Make sure you can access behavioural data that these platforms can use to tailor thumbnails (e.g., Google Analytics).

Setup and Integration:

8. **Platform Signup**: Register and complete the setup process on your chosen platform.

9. **Content Management System (CMS) Integration**: Link the AI platform with your existing CMS (like WordPress or Joomla) if applicable.

10. **Initial Configuration**: Set your objectives and target audience within the platform's dashboard for more tailored thumbnails.

Testing:

11. **Test Runs**: Use the platform's test feature, if available, to see what kinds of thumbnails are generated.

12. **A/B Testing**: Many platforms offer built-in A/B testing. Use this to compare AI-generated thumbnails with your existing ones.

Optimisation:

13. **Real-Time Adjustments**: Platforms like TubeBuddy offer real-time adjustments. Enable this feature for continual thumbnail optimisation.

14. **Quality and Ethics Review**: Periodically check to ensure thumbnails meet quality and ethical standards.

Reporting and Analytics:

15. **In-Platform Metrics**: Use the analytics provided by the platform to track key performance indicators like CTR, viewer retention, and user engagement.

16. **Strategy Adjustment**: Based on the analytics, adjust your objectives and optimisation methods as needed.

Ongoing Management:

17. **Platform Updates**: Keep an eye on any updates or new features rolled out by the platform.

18. **Compliance Checks**: Stay updated with ethical and compliance guidelines to ensure your thumbnails remain above board.

19. **Periodic Review**: Regularly check the performance of your AI-generated thumbnails and make adjustments as necessary.

Chapter 11: Transforming Vertical Video Marketing with Artificial Intelligence

In traditional vertical video marketing, the challenges often revolve around resource-intensive tasks such as video production, subtitling, and analytics.

For instance, manually producing high-quality videos demands a considerable investment of time and money, often requiring a skilled team to handle various elements like camera control, lighting, and editing.

Subtitling is another hurdle; it's laborious to transcribe and translate content for international audiences manually. Furthermore, gathering and interpreting video analytics to understand viewer behaviour can be complex and time-consuming.

Enter Artificial Intelligence: a game-changing technology that significantly lowers these barriers. With AI, even a small business or a one-person team can automate camera controls, generate subtitles, and obtain in-depth analytics with ease and at a fraction of the traditional cost.

By simplifying these intricate processes, AI is democratising the vertical video marketing landscape, making it accessible for businesses of all sizes.

In the digital age, where the consumer's attention span is fleeting and competition is fierce, staying at the forefront of technological innovation is vital. In particular, the ubiquity of smartphones has shifted the video format landscape dramatically towards vertical videos. Gone are the days when horizontal videos ruled the marketing world. Today, vertical videos are an increasingly dominant force that marketers can ill afford to ignore. This shift is not merely cosmetic; it offers tangible benefits by significantly boosting user engagement and thereby maximising both conversion rates and profits.

Artificial Intelligence (AI) is another transformative force converging with the trend towards vertical videos, creating a synergy that is redefining the way we look at digital marketing. With its ability to streamline operations and remove the tedium from several aspects of video production, AI is truly a game-changer. One pertinent example is the use of AI to control cameras and lighting conditions. Imagine shooting a promotional video and not having to worry about readjusting lights or refocusing cameras—AI algorithms take care of these tasks in real-time, eliminating the need for constant human supervision and thereby enhancing operational efficiency.

In this comprehensive chapter, we'll probe further into the fascinating, fast-evolving domain of AI-powered vertical video marketing. We will dissect its colossal impact on content creation, the nuances of audience targeting, and its increasingly important role in the broader digital marketing ecosystem.

11.1 Analytics, Video Length, and Engagement Patterns Through AI

Navigating today's marketplace is akin to venturing into a jungle teeming with competition. As such, numerous companies across sectors are deploying AI technologies to manage their video content more effectively and stand out from the crowd. One of the critical areas where AI lends a helping hand is in the assessment of the ideal video length.

Determining the optimal video length isn't a one-size-fits-all exercise; it's contingent on multiple variables like the video's purpose, its position within the sales funnel, and its target demographic. However, one golden rule is crystal clear: videos need to capture the audience's attention immediately and sustain it. If a video doesn't engage a viewer within the first few seconds, chances are, that viewer will move on, thereby negating any potential conversion opportunity.

Let's delve into some platform-specific examples to illustrate this point:

- **Facebook**: This social media juggernaut has seen a meteoric rise in video content. Marketers have quickly caught on, utilising videos to connect with audiences effectively. Here, shorter videos, often less than two minutes, tend to perform better because they fit neatly into the fast-scrolling behaviour of users.

- **Instagram**: Known for its emphasis on visual aesthetics, Instagram demands high-quality video content. Brands often use visually striking, 15-second videos in Instagram Stories to make an immediate impact.

AI's role in video analytics is multidimensional, and its contributions are felt across a variety of applications:

- **Object Detection**: For example, in a retail scenario, AI could automatically recognise and count the number of people entering and exiting a store, providing insights into customer footfall and potential conversion rates.

- **Object Segmentation**: In the automotive industry, autonomous vehicles use AI to identify and classify objects, differentiating between pedestrians, other vehicles, and obstacles. This level of accuracy is critical for safe and efficient operation.

- **Object Tracking**: Within sports analytics, AI has revolutionised how we consume sports entertainment. For instance, during a football match, AI can track players and the ball to give viewers insightful real-time statistics, such as possession time or distance covered by individual players.

- **Content Type and Audience Analysis**: In the entertainment sector, streaming services like Netflix use AI to categorise their vast libraries into genres and sub-genres. This level of classification helps in recommending the right kind of content to the right audience, increasing viewer engagement and, consequently, subscription rates.

By employing AI in these analytical ways, we're not merely automating processes; we're extracting deeper insights than ever before, fine-tuning our content strategies, and, ultimately, driving greater value for our businesses and our audiences alike.

11.2 AI-Enabled Translation of Video Captions and Subtitles

Subtitles are more than a mere add-on; they are a vital component of video content that significantly influences user engagement, accessibility, and SEO performance. The traditional process of generating subtitles is a meticulous, labour-intensive exercise that involves transcription, timing, and translation.

With the advent of AI technologies, this process has undergone a profound transformation, becoming far more efficient and scalable.

How to Utilise AI for Subtitles:

- **Upload Video and Transcribe**: AI tools like Google's AutoML or IBM Watson can automatically transcribe the spoken words in your video into text. For example, a marketing video highlighting a new tech product can have its technical jargon automatically converted into written words, making it more comprehensible.

- **Preview in Editor**: After transcription, most AI platforms offer a visual editor where you can fine-tune the automatically generated captions. This is especially crucial for content where timing is essential, such as instructional videos or live performances.

- **Translate Captions**: One of the standout capabilities of AI is its ability to translate these transcriptions into numerous languages in real-time. For a global brand, this means you can immediately reach non-English-speaking demographics, like Spanish speakers in the U.S. or Mandarin speakers in China, without needing to hire multiple translators.

- **Export and Embed**: The last step is to embed these AI-generated captions into your video. Software like Adobe Premiere Pro can integrate these captions seamlessly, ensuring they align perfectly with the video timeline.

Benefits of Embedding Subtitles:

- **Reaching a Wider Audience**: The accessibility factor cannot be overstated. Subtitles cater to a diverse range of viewers, including those who are hearing-impaired and those who may be watching the video in a noisy environment or a setting where audio is not feasible.

- **Improved SEO**: Platforms like YouTube use AI algorithms to scan, index, and rank videos based, in part, on their subtitle content. This is a boon for video discoverability, enhancing its likelihood to appear in search results and thereby potentially increasing viewer count.

- **Enhanced Retention**: Cognitive science suggests that the process of engaging with both audio and text can improve retention of the content. For educational or instructional videos, this can be particularly beneficial as it enhances the learning experience.

- **Increased Engagement**: Metrics such as "likes," "shares," and viewing duration are the lifeblood of digital marketing. Subtitles contribute to these KPIs by making the video content more digestible and easier to follow, thereby encouraging longer viewing times and higher rates of engagement.

Challenges in Using AI for Subtitles:

While AI tools offer considerable advantages, they are not without their drawbacks. One such limitation is the inability to capture the nuanced facets of human communication, such as sarcasm, emotional inflections, or cultural idioms. These are areas where human translation and transcription still hold a competitive edge. Moreover, inconsistencies in captioning guidelines across different platforms can pose a challenge in maintaining uniform quality and compliance.

Conclusion

The integration of AI into vertical video marketing signifies a lot more than mere feature enhancement; it embodies a radical shift in the conception, development, and promotion of digital content. From automating the laborious aspects of video production to offering deep, data-driven insights into viewer interactions, AI stands as a revolutionary force. This is not a fleeting trend but a seismic shift that is poised to redefine the contours of digital marketing in a way that's both impactful and enduring.

Chapter 12: Limitations and Challenges

In the realm of video marketing, the traditional challenges have been manifold: from the costs associated with producing high-quality videos and the complexities of analytics to the painstaking effort needed for things like subtitles and object recognition.

These barriers often made effective video marketing a field dominated by those with deep pockets and specialized skills. However, the advent of AI technology has started to level the playing field. While it may not eliminate all barriers—financial, ethical, or technical—it certainly lowers them substantially.

This chapter will delve into the limitations and challenges that still exist when implementing AI in video marketing, offering a nuanced view of its potential to democratise the industry.

The adoption of artificial intelligence (AI) in vertical video marketing offers boundless potential, from automating menial tasks to providing deep, actionable insights. However, it would be remiss to overlook the technology's shortcomings and the challenges that come with its implementation. This chapter seeks to elucidate the limitations of AI in video marketing while offering a balanced perspective on its utility.

12.1 Limitations of AI in Video Marketing

Data Dependency and Bias

AI's efficacy is intrinsically tied to the data it is trained on. Both the quantity and quality of this data matter; poor or biased data can skew the AI's analytics, making its outputs unreliable or even counterproductive.

Example

Suppose an AI algorithm responsible for video analytics is trained primarily on action-packed video game trailers aimed at a young demographic. If you were to use this same algorithm to assess the performance of a DIY gardening video aimed at older adults, the insights would likely be inaccurate or misleading. The algorithm could, for instance, misinterpret long pauses as 'boring' periods rather than moments of contemplation or admiration for the content being presented.

Interpretation of Human Nuances

One of AI's most notable limitations is its current inability to fully comprehend the subtleties of human emotion, tone, and context. This shortcoming becomes evident when using AI to auto-generate subtitles, which may omit these important aspects and lead to misunderstandings.

Example

If a speaker in a video uses sarcasm, the automated subtitle may not capture this, leading viewers to take the statement literally. The difference between "Great job" said sincerely and "Great job" said sarcastically is lost on most AI, yet it significantly changes the message.

High Initial Costs

The initial investment required for setting up an AI-driven video marketing system can be hefty. The cost for software licenses, hardware, and potentially hiring experts for setup and maintenance can add up quickly.

Example

A start-up company looking to venture into vertical video marketing may find it financially straining to invest in top-tier AI solutions like IBM Watson or Adobe Sensei for video analytics and object recognition. Much of this can now be overcome with 'all-in-one' platforms readily available nowadays.

Ethical Concerns

Utilising AI in video marketing also brings up a slew of ethical issues, particularly concerning data privacy and surveillance. Marketers need to be extremely cautious about how they collect and use data, ensuring that they abide by laws and regulations.

Example

Using AI algorithms to analyse in-store customer behaviour via surveillance cameras could lead to privacy issues. This technology could inadvertently capture sensitive information, leading to ethical and legal ramifications.

Technical Limitations

While AI technology continues to advance at a rapid pace, it still has limitations in terms of its reliability and accuracy. Bugs and technical glitches can occur, which could hamper your marketing campaign.

Example

You might face a situation where your AI-driven object detection system wrongly identifies a featured product in your retail video, causing it to be mislabelled. Such a mistake could misinform your audience and negatively impact your campaign's efficacy.

By considering these limitations and being prepared to address them, marketers can implement AI solutions more thoughtfully and effectively. Being forewarned is forearmed; understanding AI's limitations helps you get the best out of its capabilities while mitigating risks.

12.2 Troubleshooting and Common Pitfalls

Navigating the challenges and pitfalls of employing AI in video marketing is crucial for ensuring that the technology serves its intended purpose effectively. Let's delve into some common problems and solutions for better preparedness.

- **Inaccurate Analytics**

Problem

Your AI-driven analytics dashboard shows inconsistent or puzzling data, such as unexpected spikes or drops in viewer engagement.

Solution

Always validate your data source before training your AI algorithms. Check for any biases or limitations in the data sets, and ensure they are comprehensive and representative of your target audience.

Example

If your analytics indicate a sudden increase in engagement that doesn't align with any marketing initiatives, your data may be skewed or incomplete. This could be due to the AI algorithm being trained on a limited or biased data set, such as only weekend data when you also need weekday insights.

- **Subtitle Synchronisation**

Problem

The automated subtitles generated by AI are not synchronising properly with the video dialogue, causing confusion among viewers.

Solution

Either manually adjust the time-stamps for the subtitles or opt for a more reliable AI transcription service that has better synchronisation capabilities.

Example

If you notice that the subtitles appear a second or two after the dialogue in a training video, it can break the viewer's concentration and result in poor understanding of the content. Switching to a more accurate AI service like Rev.com could solve this issue.

- **High Operational Costs**

Problem

The financial burden of implementing and maintaining state-of-the-art AI tools is stretching your budget thin.

Solution

You may want to consider cost-effective, open-source AI options. Alternatively, you could phase the implementation to spread out the expenses over a longer time frame.

Example

If you find that Adobe Sensei is costing more than it's bringing in value, you might consider open-source alternatives like TensorFlow for certain AI tasks to lessen the financial impact.

- **Video Content Misclassification**

Problem

The AI algorithm is incorrectly categorising the genre or theme of the videos you upload, which affects SEO and targeting.

Solution

Make it a habit to periodically review and if necessary, manually adjust the video classification settings on your AI marketing tool.

Example

If your educational video on 'sustainable living' is being miscategorised as 'entertainment,' it may not reach the intended audience looking for informative content on sustainability.

- **Audience Engagement Drop**

Problem

Despite the AI integrations, you observe a drop in key audience engagement metrics like viewing time or social shares.

Solution

Re-examine your engagement analytics and content strategies. The content itself, or the way it's being presented, may need to be realigned with your target audience's interests and expectations.

Example

If you notice a declining trend in viewer engagement despite using AI tools, it might indicate that the AI recommendations are not resonating with your target audience. You may need to tweak the algorithms or bring in a human touch to connect better with your audience.

AI's transformative influence on vertical video marketing is undeniable, but it is not without its shortcomings and challenges. Equipped with the knowledge of these potential pitfalls and their solutions, marketers can wield AI technology more judiciously, maximising its benefits while minimising its limitations. Being proactive in troubleshooting will go a long way in crafting more effective and targeted video marketing campaigns.

In the fast-paced world of video marketing, staying ahead of the curve has always been a challenge. Traditional methods required substantial resources—both time and money—to analyse market trends, viewer behaviour, and the effectiveness of different video formats.

This placed smaller businesses and individual marketers at a disadvantage, making it difficult for them to compete with larger organisations equipped with more robust resources. However, the advent of AI is rapidly changing this landscape.

This chapter delves into the future trends in AI and video marketing that promise to further lower these barriers. From advanced analytics tools to automated video creation, the next wave of AI innovations is set to make advanced marketing strategies more accessible than ever, allowing even the smallest players to execute sophisticated campaigns.

As we advance into a new era of digital marketing, understanding what the future holds for the integration of Artificial Intelligence (AI) and video marketing is crucial for staying ahead of the curve. This chapter will delve into the upcoming innovations in AI technology relevant to video marketing and examine their future implications for marketers and audiences alike.

13.1 Upcoming Innovations

Real-Time Personalisation

AI algorithms are becoming increasingly adept at real-time data analysis, allowing for personalised video content that caters to individual viewer preferences. For instance, AI could alter the content, format, or even the language of a video in real-time, based on a viewer's past behaviours and demographic information.

Conversational AI and Video

Incorporating AI chatbots into videos could make for a more interactive and engaging experience. Imagine a video where a virtual host could answer viewer questions in real time, guiding them through a product or a story.

Deep Learning and Video Analytics

Deep learning algorithms are expected to bring more profound insights into viewer behaviour. These advanced algorithms could analyse not just clicks and views but also more nuanced metrics like emotional responses, captured through facial recognition or speech sentiment analysis.

AI-Driven Video Creation

Upcoming AI technologies may be able to handle the entire video creation process, from conceptualisation to editing, without significant human intervention. This could democratise high-quality video production, making it accessible even to small-scale marketers.

Virtual Reality (VR) and Augmented Reality (AR) Integration

As VR and AR technologies mature, their integration with AI could offer compelling immersive experiences. Picture a shopping experience where AI-driven avatars guide you through a virtual store, with video marketing tailored to your preferences and interactions.

Ethical and Privacy Concerns

With great power comes great responsibility. The advanced capabilities of AI, especially in areas like facial recognition and data collection, raise important questions about user privacy and data security that will need to be addressed.

Job Market Disruptions

As AI takes on more roles in video production and analytics, there will likely be shifts in job roles within the industry. While some jobs may become obsolete, new roles centred around managing and interpreting AI capabilities are likely to emerge.

Accessibility and Inclusivity

The rise of AI in video marketing has the potential to make content more accessible. Features like automated subtitling and translation could make videos comprehensible to a wider, more diverse audience, breaking down language and hearing barriers.

Economic Impact

The streamlining and automating of various aspects of video marketing through AI could result in significant cost savings for businesses, potentially lowering the financial barriers to entry for startups and small businesses.

Audience Expectations

As AI-driven personalised experiences become the norm, audience expectations will also evolve. Businesses will need to continually innovate to meet these heightened expectations for customisation, interactivity, and content quality.

The future of AI and video marketing is replete with opportunities and challenges. Marketers who keep abreast of these trends and implications will be better positioned to adapt and thrive in this dynamic landscape. From offering unprecedented personalisation to raising new ethical considerations, the integration of AI into video marketing promises to be a transformative force that will reshape the industry in profound ways.

Navigating the AI-Powered Video Marketing Labyrinth: Checklists for Every Level

As video marketing continuously evolves, staying competitive means embracing the transformative power of Artificial Intelligence. Whether you're just dipping your toes into the video marketing pool or you're an experienced veteran looking to stay ahead, AI technologies offer solutions that can streamline your workflow, elevate the quality of your content, and help you engage more effectively with your audience.

Recognising that expertise in this field can vary widely, we've created three different checklists—tailored for beginners, intermediates, and advanced users—to guide you in crafting, executing, and analysing AI-powered video marketing campaigns.

These checklists offer a step-by-step approach to help you navigate the complexities of using AI in video marketing, ensuring that you're not just keeping pace with industry trends but are at the forefront of them.

Beginner's Checklist: Stepping Into AI-Powered Video Marketing

Planning

1. **Market Research**: Identify your target audience and competitors.

2. **Objective Setting**: Decide what you want to achieve (brand awareness, engagement, sales).

3. **Content Ideation**: Brainstorm topics and formats (tutorials, testimonials, product showcases).

Production

4. **Storyboarding**: Create a simple storyboard for your video content.

5. **Camera Setup**: Use smartphones or basic cameras; AI can enhance video quality in post-production.

6. **Lighting**: Make sure your lighting is adequate; consider natural light or basic lighting kits.

Post-production

7. **Basic Editing**: Use beginner-friendly tools like iMovie.

8. **Transcription**: Utilise AI services like Descript to auto-generate subtitles.

9. **SEO Basics**: Incorporate keywords in your video title and description.

Analytics

10. **Basic Metrics**: Track views, likes, and shares using built-in analytics on platforms like YouTube or Facebook.

Intermediate Checklist: Elevating Your AI-Powered Video Marketing Game

Planning

1. **SWOT Analysis**: Conduct a detailed SWOT analysis focusing on video marketing.

2. **Advanced Targeting**: Use AI to analyse customer personas and predict behaviour.

3. **Content Calendar**: Plan a content calendar using AI tools for optimal posting times.

Production

4. **AI for Storyboarding**: Use AI-based tools like Lumen5 for automated storyboarding.

5. **Advanced Camera Control**: Use AI algorithms for better camera control and automated lighting adjustments.

Post-production

6. **Advanced Editing**: Use software like Adobe Premiere Pro with AI plugins for smart editing.

7. **AI Transcription & Translation**: Use sophisticated AI services to auto-translate subtitles.

Analytics

8. **Deep Analytics**: Use AI tools like HubSpot to measure engagement, drop-off rates, and conversion.

Advanced Checklist: Mastering AI-Powered Video Marketing
Planning

1. **Market Prediction**: Use AI to predict market trends and demands.

2. **Dynamic Content Strategy**: Implement an AI-driven dynamic content strategy for real-time adjustments.

3. **A/B Testing**: Use AI to run A/B tests on multiple video formats and styles.

Production

4. **Automated Production**: Use AI to entirely automate video production processes.

5. **Object Tracking and Analytics**: Implement advanced object tracking features relevant to your sector.

Post-production

6. **Machine Learning Algorithms**: Utilise machine learning for highly personalised video recommendations.

7. **NLP for SEO**: Employ Natural Language Processing (NLP) algorithms for superior SEO strategies.

Analytics

8. **Predictive Analytics**: Leverage AI to predict future performance metrics and make real-time adjustments.

By following these checklists, you can gradually build up your proficiency in using AI for video marketing, starting from the basics and moving all the way up to highly advanced strategies.

As we bring this exploration of AI in vertical video marketing to a close, it's important to remember that we are at the nexus of a seismic shift in how digital marketing will be conducted in the years to come. From the mechanics of video production to intricate audience analytics and from translation capabilities to ethical considerations, AI is setting the pace for industry-wide transformation.

This book aimed to offer a comprehensive guide that not only introduced the marvels of integrating AI but also presented a balanced view by highlighting its limitations and challenges. Moreover, with the tailored checklists provided, we hope you have a ready reckoner for implementing these advancements at whatever stage you find yourself in your journey.

While this book aimed to be exhaustive, it's worth remembering that we're in an evolving landscape. Technologies will continue to improve, bringing in new tools and possibilities. Future trends could involve AI systems capable of generating entire marketing campaigns, from video creation to deployment, that are tailored to an individual's preferences. As data collection becomes more sophisticated, the ethical considerations surrounding it will become even more critical. Navigating this complex terrain will require not just technological acumen but also moral and ethical responsibility.

If this book has done its job well, you're now itching to put all these insights into practice. Start small if you're a beginner, perhaps by implementing AI-powered analytics to understand your current audience better. For those with intermediate expertise, delve into automated video creation and subtitle translations to reach a broader audience. Advanced users can explore real-time content adjustments based on real-time analytics or delve into predictive modelling to foresee future trends.

The stage is now set for you to play your part in this ever-evolving narrative. As you embark on or continue your journey in AI-driven vertical video marketing, remember that the only constant is change. Your ability to adapt, scale, and innovate will determine your success in this exciting, challenging field.

So go ahead, dive into the brave new world of AI-driven video marketing. Your audience awaits you, and the future is yours to shape.

Thank you for investing your time in this book. Here's to your forthcoming success!

www.ingramcontent.com/pod-product-compliance
Lightning Source LLC
Chambersburg PA
CBHW062253290526
45794CB00006B/2529